MIRACLES OF CARD PLAY

'*Miracles of Card Play* attains a new high in entertainment for players at all levels as they follow the exploits of the bridge-playing monks of St Titus who, led by their formidable Abbot, are involved in the Gold Cup, the Hubert Phillips Bowl, the National inter-monastery championship, and a mission to darkest Africa to convert the Bozwambi tribe to the Acol system. Marvellous fun.'
– Eric Bowtell, *Oxford Times*

'Something you must not miss is *Miracles of Card Play* by David Bird and Terence Reese. Not only are the hands ingeniously constructed, but the narrative is extremely amusing.'

– Pat Cotter, *Country Life*

Miracles of Card Play

TERENCE REESE and DAVID BIRD

VICTOR GOLLANCZ
in association with
PETER CRAWLEY

First published in Great Britain 1982
in association with Peter Crawley
by Victor Gollancz Ltd
Reprinted 1984
First paperback edition published 1989
Third impression 1998
in association with Peter Crawley
by Victor Gollancz
An imprint of the Cassell Group
Wellington House, 125 Strand, London WC2R 0BB

A catalogue record for this book is available from
the British Library

ISBN 0 575 06594 X

Printed in Great Britain by
St Edmundsbury Press Ltd, Bury St Edmunds, Suffolk

Contents

Contents

Foreword

by Terence Reese

Some of the stories in this book have appeared in bridge magazines round the world. Our thanks are due to the editors of *Bridge Magazine*, *Bridge World*, *Australian Bridge*, *New Zealand Bridge*, and *South African Bulletin*, for permission to reprint.

Lynx-eyed readers will have noted that the original stories were written by David Bird alone. I liked them very much and suggested that we work together on a book. Many twists have been added to the narrative, and not a little vinegar to the dialogue. In the end it has been a combined operation – a most evil connivance by de two white bwanas, as the witch-doctor might say.

PRINCIPAL PLAYERS

At the Monastery of St. Titus

The Abbot: A capable but uninspired player; greatly jealous of his reputation.

Brother Lucius: The monastery's chief accountant and its most cunning and deceptive card-player.

Brother Xavier: Monastery barber for the past twenty years; an admirer of Brother Lucius and a good player.

Brother Anthony: Member of the silent Eustacian order and therefore, of necessity, an over-cautious bidder.

Brother Aelred: The monastery organist; a weak but aspiring player.

Brother Damien: A promising postulant, keen to make his mark on the monastery bridge scene.

Brother Fabius: The monastery pig-farmer and a sound player.

Brother Paulo: An Italian monk transferred to St. Titus to strengthen the monastery first team.

In the African Jungle

Brother Tobias: Head of the team of missionaries trying to convert the Bozwambi tribe to the Acol system.

Brother Luke: Right-hand man of Brother Tobias, but his keenest rival at the table.

The Witch-doctor: A wild overbidder, much feared by the other natives who never dare double him.

Mbozi: Docile and lazy during the play of the hand but extremely fierce in the post-mortem.

PART I

At the Monastery of St. Titus

1

Brother Damien's Debut

Brother Damien's heart skipped a beat as he saw the tall black-cassocked figure approach the table. Tonight was to be his first rubber in partnership with the Abbot, a significant milestone in every postulant's life. Rather like a matador making his first appearance in Madrid, Brother Damien was expected to put up an excellent performance, and several monks had gathered round the table to witness this important occasion.

"A good evening to you all," said the Abbot, who seemed in quite a tolerant mood. "You have studied my methods, I take it, Brother er . . .?"

"Brother Damien, Abbot. Yes, I hope I won't forget anything."

The Abbot subjected the cards to an unusually fierce riffle, and Brother Damien cut for North to deal the hands overleaf:

Love all, dealer North

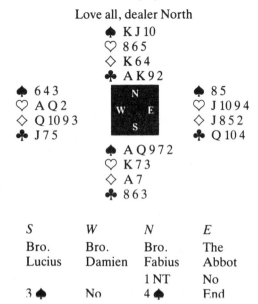

```
                ♠ K J 10
                ♡ 8 6 5
                ◇ K 6 4
                ♣ A K 9 2
  ♠ 6 4 3                        ♠ 8 5
  ♡ A Q 2          N             ♡ J 10 9 4
  ◇ Q 10 9 3    W     E          ◇ J 8 5 2
  ♣ J 7 5          S             ♣ Q 10 4
                ♠ A Q 9 7 2
                ♡ K 7 3
                ◇ A 7
                ♣ 8 6 3
```

S	W	N	E
Bro.	Bro.	Bro.	The
Lucius	Damien	Fabius	Abbot
		1 NT	No
3 ♠	No	4 ♠	End

Hoping he looked less nervous than he felt, Brother Damien opted for a safe trump lead, which was captured on the table. Brother Lucius, the acknowledged champion of the monastery rubber bridge tables, surveyed the dummy coldly, his features as impassive as ever. If clubs were 3–3 he could establish a discard, but the club trick must be lost to West, if possible, to prevent a heart lead through the king. Brother Lucius nodded to himself. Yes, he must lead twice towards the club honours to prevent West unblocking from Q x x. If no solace came from the clubs he would have to rely on the ace of hearts being well placed.

Most of the monastery's leading players would have been well satisfied with this analysis, but not Brother Lucius. A past master at increasing his chances by luring defenders into error, he led a small diamond from the table.

The Abbot followed carelessly with a small card and Brother Lucius gratefully covered it with his seven. West returned a trump but nothing could now stop declarer from discarding a club on the diamond king and ruffing the thirteenth club good. Brother Damien, who had spotted the Abbot's error, maintained a tactful silence. Perhaps the damage could be repaired on the next hand.

N–S game, dealer East

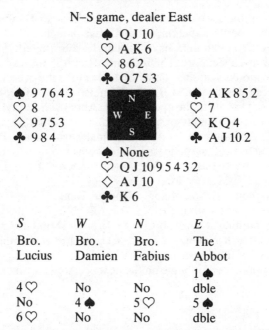

	♠ Q J 10	
	♡ A K 6	
	◇ 8 6 2	
	♣ Q 7 5 3	

♠ 9 7 6 4 3		♠ A K 8 5 2
♡ 8		♡ 7
◇ 9 7 5 3		◇ K Q 4
♣ 9 8 4		♣ A J 10 2

	♠ None	
	♡ Q J 10 9 5 4 3 2	
	◇ A J 10	
	♣ K 6	

S	W	N	E
Bro.	Bro.	Bro.	The
Lucius	Damien	Fabius	Abbot
			1 ♠
4 ♡	No	No	dble
No	4 ♠	5 ♡	5 ♠
6 ♡	No	No	dble

No one round the table had much idea who could make what, and the bidding consequently drifted somewhat high. The Abbot closed the auction with a sharp double, and Brother Damien led the four of spades to the queen and ace, which declarer ruffed. Brother Lucius crossed to the ace of trumps and led a small club which the Abbot had to duck, since otherwise declarer would have had two black suit discards for his diamonds. Winning the king of clubs, Brother Lucius returned to the heart king to lead a second spade, which was covered and ruffed. Entering dummy with the six of hearts, declarer discarded his remaining club on the established spade and led a diamond, hoping to find East with either a doubleton honour or both the outstanding honours. His prayers were answered, and the rubber that meant so much to Brother Damien drew to a tragic close.

"What an appalling lead, Brother Dunstan!" cried the Abbot.

"It's Brother Damien, Abbot," came the subdued reply.

"Well, whatever your name is, have you never heard of a Lightner double? On a diamond lead, or even on a trump lead for that matter, the slam has absolutely no chance."

"A Lightner double, Abbot?" replied Brother Damien. "After such a competitive auction, I should have thought . . ."

"Yes. You SHOULD have thought!" interrupted the Abbot, looking up expectantly. This was one of the Abbot's favourite jokes and the monks standing round the table broke into a dutiful titter.

A hush descended as Brother Damien dared to reply. "What happens if you duck the opening lead, Abbot?" he asked.

The wheels of analysis spun round in the Abbot's head, but he could find no way now for declarer to make his contract. The winner provided by the first spade trick would come too soon for declarer to make an effective discard. Whether he threw a club or a diamond he would be left with two losers.

"Did you say something, Brother Damien?" he replied, a dangerous glint in his eye.

"No, nothing at all, Abbot," said Brother Damien hastily.

At least he had managed to extract some sort of triumph from the wreckage of the disastrous rubber. And he had a feeling the Abbot would remember his name on the next occasion they met.

2

The Abbot's Practice Session

"A most exhilarating and inspiring toccata, Brother Aelred," declared the Abbot as he left the chapel after evensong.

"I must agree," added Brother Lucius. "A superb rendering with some particularly crisp work on the pedals."

"I'm glad you liked it," said Brother Aelred, somewhat overwhelmed by such unaccustomed praise. "It's got five flats in it, you know. I've been practising that last part all week."

"I feel so uplifted by it," continued the Abbot, "that I shall spend the evening engaged in some charitable work. Perhaps I'll go and visit the old folk's home down in the village."

"What an excellent idea, Abbot. I think I'll join you," said Brother Lucius, as the three of them stepped onto the close-cropped grass of the quadrangle. "Or shall we have a game?"

"Very well," said the Abbot. "I can always go down there tomorrow night instead, I suppose."

"We've got that rearranged league match on then."

"Is that tomorrow?" asked the Abbot, looking surprised. "Oh well, we'd better have a practice session now in that case."

E–W game, dealer East

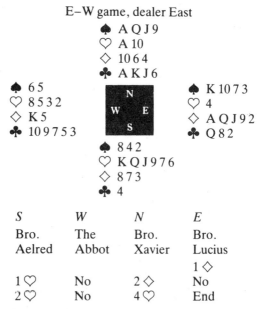

S	W	N	E
Bro.	The	Bro.	Bro.
Aelred	Abbot	Xavier	Lucius
			1 ◇
1 ♡	No	2 ◇	No
2 ♡	No	4 ♡	End

The Abbot led the king of diamonds and Brother Lucius, sitting East, overtook and cashed two more rounds. Every card remaining in his hand was a potentially dangerous exit, but a trump seemed to be the least risk. Brother Aelred won with dummy's ace and drew trumps, leaving these cards outstanding:

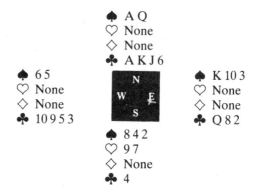

It was clear, even to Brother Aelred, that the opening bid marked both the missing black honours offside. On the nine of trumps he

[14]

threw the queen of spades from dummy and Brother Lucius, who had previously thrown a devious seven of spades, continued the good work with a deceitful ten.

It now seemed quite obvious to Brother Aelred that East had been forced to bare the spade king in order to keep his club queen sufficiently attended to prevent it being ruffed down. He crossed to dummy's ace of spades and waited expectantly for the ermine-garbed figure of the king to appear from East. It was not to be. Brother Lucius flipped a mean-looking spade three onto the table, and the contract was one down.

"Did you notice my seven of clubs, partner?" demanded the Abbot. "Declarer was bound to miscount the suit."

"It wasn't your card that put me off, Abbot," said Brother Aelred tactlessly. "It was Brother Lucius's ten of spades."

"You should have made the contract anyway," declared the Abbot. "Why didn't you play off the ace of spades at trick five before returning to hand to draw trumps? Then there's no guess to make. If Lucius keeps one of his high spades you can drop his queen of clubs."

"I still don't see what difference that makes," protested Brother Aelred. "If I cashed the ace of spades then I wouldn't be able to . . ."

The Abbot suddenly stood up, his limited supply of patience exhausted.

"I can feel an overwhelming desire for a glass of sherry coming on," he announced, sliding back an oak panel in the wall to reveal what must have been a good dozen bottles of Brother Michael's finest chickweed and burdock dry sherry.

"Got any spare glasses?" asked Brother Xavier boldly.

"Oh, very well. Help yourselves to a glass each," grunted the Abbot. "Just one, mind you. My supply is running a bit short. Now let's get on with the game."

N–S game, dealer South

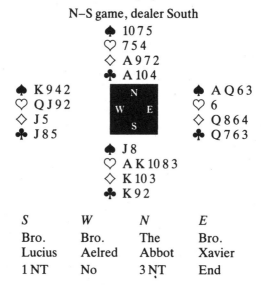

```
                    ♠ 10 7 5
                    ♡ 7 5 4
                    ◇ A 9 7 2
                    ♣ A 10 4
    ♠ K 9 4 2          N            ♠ A Q 6 3
    ♡ Q J 9 2     W         E       ♡ 6
    ◇ J 5              S            ◇ Q 8 6 4
    ♣ J 8 5                         ♣ Q 7 6 3
                    ♠ J 8
                    ♡ A K 10 8 3
                    ◇ K 10 3
                    ♣ K 9 2
```

S	W	N	E
Bro.	Bro.	The	Bro.
Lucius	Aelred	Abbot	Xavier
1 NT	No	3 NT	End

Brother Lucius took a sip of his sherry, nodded appreciatively at its well-rounded flavour, and opened a 16–18 no-trump. He reckoned his hand was worth 14 points in high cards, plus one for the two tens, and at least one for the long hearts.

The Abbot raised him briskly to game. He gave no consideration to bidding just two no-trumps; this was unthinkable with 8 points, two tens, and Brother Aelred on lead.

Brother Aelred placed the queen of hearts hopefully on the table, and the Abbot displayed his meagre dummy. Brother Lucius contributed a cunning eight of hearts to the first trick and Brother Aelred, surprised that he seemed to have found a good lead for a change, continued innocently with another heart.

Declarer had bolstered his total to eight tricks without much trouble, but a ninth trick was clearly going to be hard to come by. Hoping something would develop, he cashed out the heart suit, throwing a diamond and a spade from dummy. East parted with one diamond and two clubs, but he could not afford a third club or his partner's knave would become exposed to a finesse. His fourth discard therefore had to be a spade.

Brother Aelred, who still looked rather pale after seeing his partner show out of hearts at trick 2, was in a similar position. Since he had to keep two diamonds to protect his partner's queen from a

[16]

finesse, he too had to discard a spade. The outstanding spades were now divided 3–3 and Brother Lucius exited in spades, hoping that the defence would present him with a ninth trick in the minors. When West won the third round of spades, on which declarer threw a diamond from dummy and a club from hand, this was the strangely symmetrical end position:

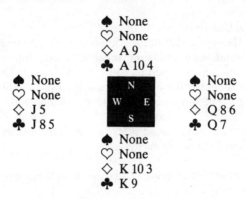

Brother Aelred, sitting West, fingered each of his cards in turn, but whichever suit he chose, and whether he played a small card or an honour, declarer could succeed by playing for split honours. Eventually Brother Aelred tried the eight of clubs. Brother Lucius put the finishing touches to a stylish performance by guessing the suit correctly and capturing the remaining tricks.

"Is it any good if I hold on to my guard in both the minors?" asked Brother Xavier. "Then Brother Aelred can afford to keep four spades."

"Hmm. If you do that I think I'd have to throw a second diamond earlier and keep three spades to the ten in dummy," replied Brother Lucius, consulting the ceiling learnedly. "To hold on to both minors you'd have to come down to ace doubleton of spades, and then the spade suit would be blocked."

"Quite so. If I hadn't held the ten of spades I wouldn't have given you 3 NT," observed the Abbot.

3

The Abbot Digs for Gold

"Henry, it's come!" Mrs. Blott shouted excitedly up the stairs.

"What's come?"

"The Gold Cup draw. Shall I open it?"

"No, no. Hang on a minute. I've nearly finished shaving."

Mr. Blott sat down at the family breakfast table, ripped open the brown envelope and scanned its contents anxiously. "How amazing!" he exclaimed. "It's a home draw against an Abbot Hugo Yorke-Smith of the Monastery of St. Titus in Hampshire."

"Good heavens!" replied his wife. "You'll have to hide those magazines of yours. And what shall I do for refreshments? Brown bread and a carafe of water each?"

Two weeks later the monastery first team was ushered into the Blotts' front living-room.

"And er ... which one of you is the Abbot?" asked Mr. Blott, surveying the four monks, who were resplendent in their purple shirts and crisply laundered black habits.

"I have that honour," declared the Abbot coldly. "Shall we toss?"

E–W game, dealer West

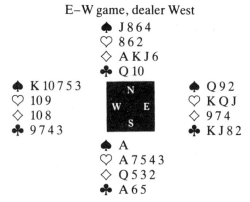

[18]

The Abbot Digs for Gold

Room 1:	S	W	N	E
	Mr.	Bro.	Mrs.	Bro.
	Blott	Fabius	Blott	Lucius
		No	No	No
	1 ♡	No	1 ♠	No
	2 ♢	No	3 ♡	No
	4 ♡	End		

Brother Fabius led the ten of hearts to the knave, and declarer ducked. Winning the king of hearts return, Mr. Blott puffed thoughtfully at his pipe. Somehow he had to take care of his third club. One plan was to play a small club towards the table and guess which card to put up. If he guessed wrongly and East won, he would still be safe if East did not have the last trump. However, an opening lead from Q 10 9 of trumps could be ruled out, so surely East must hold the missing trump.

In an uncharacteristic flash of inspiration Mr. Blott hit upon a superior line. He crossed to the ace of diamonds and, smiling reassuringly at his wife, led the queen of clubs from the table. Now he would be safe if West held either club honour, since he could lose the club trick to the hand that did not contain the outstanding trump.

Mrs. Blott failed to return her husband's smile when East turned up with both club honours and duly removed dummy's last trump to defeat the contract.

"Can I make it on that trump lead?" enquired Mr. Blott, scratching his forehead.

"Evidently not," replied Brother Lucius.

Room 2:	S	W	N	E
	Bro.	Amanda	The	Mrs.
	Xavier	Blott	Abbot	Bucket
		No	No	1 NT
	2 ♣	No	3 ♡	No
	4 ♡	End		

Mrs. Bucket, whose dummy play rarely justified her extremely forward bidding, opened the auction with a weak no-trump, but the monastery pair soon sniffed out the heart game with an Astro sequence. Mrs. Bucket led the king of trumps, and once more declarer ducked and won the trump continuation. The Abbot now cashed the ace of spades, came to hand with the knave of diamonds and ruffed a spade. He then returned to hand with the king of diamonds and ruffed a second spade. Overtaking dummy's queen of diamonds with the ace from hand, the Abbot placed his last spade on the baize.

East could only discard a club, and the Abbot ruffed in dummy for the third time. It was clear now that East's last four cards were the queen of trumps and three clubs to the king, so the Abbot crossed back to his six of diamonds and threw East in to lead away from the king of clubs.

"An exquisite overtrick, Abbot," exclaimed Brother Xavier.

"Yes, a dummy reversal in the auction and a dummy reversal in the play!" chortled the Abbot. "Make a note of the hand, will you, for our next bulletin?"

The monastery team continued to play well and with only eight hands left they led by 46 IMPs.

"Well, thank you," said the Abbot, feeling for his car keys. "It has been a most enjoyable game."

"It's not over yet," snapped Mr. Blott. "My wife and I will play East–West in this room. It's your choice."

The final set began disastrously for the monastery team. Brother Fabius failed to locate the trump queen in a thin diamond slam, while in the other room Mrs. Blott coasted home in 3 NT. Two boards later Brother Lucius went one down in a spade game, playing for a squeeze, and lost 13 IMPs when Mr. Blott played for the finesse instead.

With the state of the match in mind, both sides spotted the heart slam on the following hand.

N–S game, dealer West

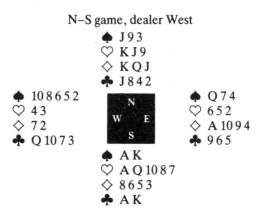

The Abbot Digs for Gold

Room 1:	S	W	N	E
	The	Mr.	Bro.	Mrs.
	Abbot	Blott	Xavier	Blott
		No	No	No
	1 ♡	No	3 ♡	No
	6 ♡	End		

Mr. Blott led the seven of diamonds to the king and ace, and the Abbot won East's club return. The hand offered several possibilities and the Abbot, who was feeling the effect of Mr. Blott's gas-fire, sat back in his chair to consider them.

What about a dummy reversal? This would involve taking three ruffs in the South hand. The entry situation, and the diamond lead, made this line of play unpromising.

An alternative was to play off four rounds of trumps, a second diamond and the top spades, playing for a minor-suit trump squeeze. This was likely to succeed if a defender with four diamonds, presumably East, held either the queen of clubs or any four clubs.

"It's your play, Abbot," said Brother Xavier.

"Yes, yes. I know," replied the Abbot, irritated at this interruption to his learned analysis.

Eventually he opted for a third line. He took one round of trumps, played off the top clubs and entered dummy with a second round of trumps to ruff a club. When the queen of clubs failed to appear, he tested the diamond suit. Mr. Blott showed out on the third round, but as his wife held the outstanding trump, the contract was home. The Abbot simply re-entered his hand to ruff the fourth round of diamonds.

The Abbot looked up at his partner, expecting some well-earned compliment on his fine play.

"Phew! That was lucky," said Brother Xavier, who had not really been following the hand. "Did you realise that there was still a trump out?"

Room 2:	S	W	N	E
	Amanda	Bro.	Mrs.	Bro.
	Blott	Fabius	Bucket	Lucius
		No	1 NT	No
	3 ♡	No	4 ♡	No
	6 ♡	End		

Once again Mrs. Bucket entered the arena armed with only an appalling 12-count, but her luck was in and the good heart slam was easily reached.

Brother Fabius led the seven of diamonds and Brother Lucius allowed dummy's knave to hold. Amanda Blott, the elder of the Blotts' two unmarried daughters, cashed the king of trumps and the two top clubs, then crossed to dummy with the knave of trumps. A club was ruffed but the queen did not appear. A diamond was taken by the ace and Brother Lucius returned his last trump to prevent a ruff of the fourth diamond. When declarer led her last trump, this was the end position:

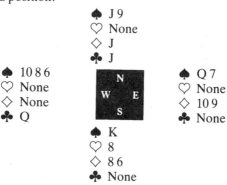

```
              ♠ J 9
              ♡ None
              ◇ J
              ♣ J
  ♠ 10 8 6              ♠ Q 7
  ♡ None      N        ♡ None
  ◇ None   W     E     ◇ 10 9
  ♣ Q         S        ♣ None
              ♠ K
              ♡ 8
              ◇ 8 6
              ♣ None
```

A club was discarded from dummy, and Brother Lucius, fearing the worst, threw a diamond. Declarer now crossed to the diamond knave and returned to the king of spades to make the last diamond.

Brother Lucius thought for a moment. "Do you know, I think I could have beaten this contract if I'd allowed the second diamond to win?" he said. "Interesting, that. Sorry, partner."

The Abbot, who had performed soundly throughout the match, listened in stony silence to the last eight results from the other room.

"I don't believe it!" he exclaimed, when the result became apparent. "How can we win by only 8 IMPs against a team of bungling novices?"

During the long drive homewards the Abbot refused to let the matter drop. "When representing the monastery, there can be no excuse for lapses of concentration," he declared, swerving violently to avoid an oncoming lorry. "None at all. Are you two in the back listening to me?"

Brother Xavier Cuts

"I had a tricky hand to bid last night on the 5p table," said Brother Aelred, settling himself down in the barber's chair. "It's game all and right-hand opponent opens one heart. What do you say on this hand?"

♠ K J 8 5 4
♡ 8 6 3
♢ Q J
♣ J 9 2

"I pass," replied Brother Xavier, a fearsome wielder of the scissors who had been monastery barber as long as anyone could remember. Rarely dwelling more than twenty seconds on a haircut, his rapid cutting action had been compared to that of an electric hedge-trimmer.

"Oh. Well, I made the perfectly reasonable overcall of one spade," said Brother Aelred. "So take it from there. Left-hand opponent doubles and your partner bids one no-trump. What do you say?"

"I pass, of course," replied Brother Xavier, who had completed the haircut and was standing back to admire his handiwork. "Would you like a shave?"

"Very well, but none of Brother Michael's rosehip and heather aftershave. I came out in a rash last week. Anyhow, getting back to the hand, since I had only eight points, no heart stop and a five-card suit, I made a weakness take-out of two spades."

Brother Xavier, who was sharpening his razor on a leather strap, winced.

"So take up the bidding from there," continued Brother Aelred.

"Left-hand opponent doubles and your partner redoubles. What do you say now?"

"You must try three clubs, I suppose."

"Exactly!" said Brother Aelred triumphantly. "Just what I did. I'm glad you agree with my bidding. Now have a go at playing the hand, and see if you can get out for less than my 1100. A trump is led, dummy has a void spade, four hearts to the . . ."

"Sorry, too many customers today," said Brother Xavier,

completing the shave with two bold strokes of the razor. "Next, please!"

Brother Lucius stepped forward.

"Hello, Lucius. Any good hands at the £1 table last night?"

"Not really. Oh well, yes, there was one interesting play hand. East opened one heart and we got to five clubs on these hands:

> ♠ A J 10 7
> ♡ A K 4
> ♢ 8 6 5
> ♣ J 10 8

> ♠ 5
> ♡ 8 3 2
> ♢ A J 2
> ♣ A Q 9 7 5 4

"The Abbot led the king of diamonds. How do you play it?"

"I'd rather be in three no-trumps," remarked Brother Xavier. "What on earth was your bidding? If South overcalls two clubs then surely North would . . ."

"The full auction need not concern us," interrupted Brother Lucius in an irritated tone. "Do you duck the diamond at trick one?"

"Yes, and since West very likely has both diamond honours, the opening bid marks East with the remaining eleven points. Anyhow, what happens next? Surely the Abbot didn't play another diamond?"

"No, he switched to a small spade."

"Right. I win, run the knave of clubs and play another club."

"Yes," replied Brother Lucius. "Clubs are 2–2 and East plays his king on the second round."

"Well, West would have led a singleton in his partner's suit, so East probably has only five hearts. I can't see any better chance than to hope that he is 3–5–3–2, in which case I can ruff out the king–queen of spades, establishing the knave."

"One down," said Brother Lucius, looking pleased.

"Well, how did you play it?" asked Brother Xavier, snipping away.

"I thought that as West was likely to be short in hearts, I would

[24]

aim to throw him in on the fourth round of spades. Then he'd have to lead a diamond into my A J or concede a ruff-and-discard.

"Oh, yes," said Brother Xavier. "So what happened?"

"When the knave of clubs held, I led the knave of spades, covered and ruffed. I then crossed to a heart and led the ten of spades, covered and ruffed. The ace of clubs felled the outstanding trumps, so I crossed to the other high heart and led the seven of spades, throwing my last heart from hand. The Abbot, sitting West, won the trick with the nine and had to lead back into my diamonds. These were the four hands:

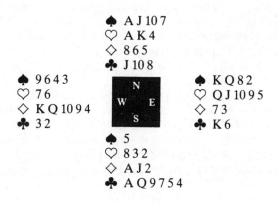

```
                        ♠ A J 10 7
                        ♡ A K 4
                        ♢ 8 6 5
                        ♣ J 10 8
  ♠ 9 6 4 3                             ♠ K Q 8 2
  ♡ 7 6              N                  ♡ Q J 10 9 5
  ♢ K Q 10 9 4   W       E              ♢ 7 3
  ♣ 3 2              S                  ♣ K 6
                        ♠ 5
                        ♡ 8 3 2
                        ♢ A J 2
                        ♣ A Q 9 7 5 4
```

"Brother Fabius, sitting East, told the Abbot he could have beaten the contract by unblocking the nine of spades. The Abbot's face went a sort of deep purple with annoyance, you know how it goes all blotchy."

"Oh, yes, I wish I'd been there to see it," said Brother Xavier, chuckling. "But surely if he does unblock, you can just ruff the fourth spade, cash the ace of diamonds and throw East in with a heart to give ruff-and-discard."

"Quite so. But that's beyond them," replied Brother Lucius with a short laugh.

Brother Xavier glanced in the mirror, and a horrific sight met his eyes. The Abbot was sitting there, waiting for a haircut and listening intently to every word.

"And to think they call themselves bridge players," continued Brother Lucius, with an amused shake of the head.

"Yes, well I've finished," said Brother Xavier, suddenly looking rather unwell. "Next, please."

Focusing an expression on Brother Lucius that resembled a black laser beam, the Abbot walked sternly forward and took his seat.

"You might have used your razor to better purpose while you had the chance," he grunted.

"Anything special for you today, Abbot?" asked Brother Xavier nervously.

"What do you suppose I want? A blue rinse and set? Short top-back-and-sides, man, you've been cutting my hair for twenty years."

The Abbot sighed and raised his voice for the benefit of the other monks awaiting a haircut. "It's sad about Brother Lucius. I used to think he was a fairly good player. But just look at that hand he was talking about; his play was wrong from the start."

"Do you mean he shouldn't have held up the ace of diamonds?" asked Brother Xavier.

"The obvious play is to contribute the knave at trick one," replied the Abbot. "West doubtless continues diamonds, and now the game cannot be beaten. Declarer simply wins and returns a third diamond, rectifying the count in preparation for a trump squeeze. Too late, West attacks the dummy's major-suit entries, but declarer runs the trump suit to leave the following position:

♠ J 10
♡ A K
♢ None
♣ None

♠ None
♡ 8 3 2
♢ None
♣ 4

"There is no guess involved on this occasion," continued the Abbot in stentorian tones. "If neither spade honour has appeared, East must be down to only two hearts. And remember, this line doesn't need the 2–2 trump break that Lucius required."

"Yes, I see. Very impressive indeed!" replied Brother Xavier, wondering how many hours of devotional time his superior had spent on this analysis. He helped the Abbot to his feet and brushed some loose hairs off his cassock. "I do hope you'll forgive us for our light-hearted banter of a few moments ago."

"Heaven preserve us," exclaimed the Abbot. "Does the elephant notice the ticks on its hide?"

5

Brother Lucius Defends

"Two clubs!" opened Brother Lucius in a deliberately intimidating voice.

"That's a normal strong opening, is it?" enquired young Brother Damien nervously.

"You mustn't ask me. Ask my partner," replied Brother Lucius.

"All right. Well, what does two clubs mean in your system?" continued Brother Damien, turning towards East, an elderly monk unknown to him. The old monk stroked his greying beard and smiled pleasantly back at him, but offered no reply. Perhaps he is a little deaf, thought Brother Damien.

"IS TWO CLUBS STRONG?" he persisted, somewhat louder than he had intended.

The group of monks kibitzing the £1 table exchanged amused smiles.

"Enough of this charade," interrupted the Abbot testily. "Brother Anthony is a member of the Eustacian order of monks, who on entering this order take a vow of everlasting silence. Those Eustacians who nevertheless play bridge and discipline themselves to refrain from bidding, whatever the temptation, are among the most respected members of our community."

"I'm so sorry, Abbot. I had no idea," replied Brother Damien, his head bowed. "Perhaps, in the circumstances, I could ask you to explain the bid to me?"

"Oh, very well. It is the Eustacian multi-coloured two club opening, which is used on about six different hand-types. Most frequently it is a weakish hand based on a five- or six-card suit. Any suit."

"I see," said Brother Damien doubtfully. "Is the bid forcing?"

The Abbot raised his eyes despairingly to the ceiling. How on earth had Brother Damien managed to slip through the notoriously severe monastery entrance examination?

"No, the bid is not forcing, nor are there any responses. If the auction is kept alive the opener's rebid specifies the hand-type. Now come on. It's your call."

Brother Lucius Defends

N–S game, dealer West

```
              ♠ K 9 4
              ♡ K Q 9 2
              ◇ A J 6 5 4
              ♣ 10
♠ 8 7 3                        ♠ 6 2
♡ 10 6 4          N            ♡ J 8 7 3
◇ K 3          W     E         ◇ 10 9 7 2
♣ A Q 7 5 4       S            ♣ 8 6 2
              ♠ A Q J 10 5
              ♡ A 5
              ◇ Q 8
              ♣ K J 9 3
```

S	W	N	E
The	Bro.	Bro.	Bro.
Abbot	Lucius	Damien	Anthony
	2 ♣[1]	dble	No
4 NT	No	5 ◇	No
6 ♠	End		

[1] Eustacian multi-coloured.

When Brother Damien doubled, the Abbot considered a penalty pass but eventually opted for a Blackwood enquiry. Learning that one of the aces was in hostile hands, he closed the auction with a bid of six spades.

Brother Lucius led a trump, won by dummy's nine, and at trick two the Abbot ran the ten of clubs. Brother Lucius won deceptively with the ace and fired back another trump. The Abbot had originally intended to follow a losing club finesse with a ruffing finesse against the ace, but now he paused to reassess the situation.

If West's opening bid were the most common type, based on a weak hand with five or six clubs, declarer could ruff out East's queen of clubs and then discard his diamond loser on dummy's heart suit. This certainly seemed the most promising line available, so the Abbot cashed the king of clubs and followed it with the knave, ruffing with the dummy's last trump when Brother Lucius played low.

Only a disappointing eight of clubs fell from East. However, it struck the Abbot that there was no need to finesse for the diamond king. If West held this card and East the queen of clubs, neither would be able to guard the heart suit when the last trump was played.

Swiftly converting his thoughts into action, the Abbot cashed the ace of diamonds, a Vienna Coup, and returned to the heart ace to run his trumps, discarding four diamonds from the table. On the final trump Brother Lucius paused, then contributed the six of hearts with a show of reluctance.

The Abbot, his face aglow with triumph, looked up to check that his masterly play was receiving the full attention of the kibitzers.

"And now, partner," he announced with the air of a magician about to pull a rabbit out of his sleeve, "kindly watch closely as I play off these last three hearts. The king drops the ten and the ... seven, and the queen drops the eight and the ... eh?"

"Having none," confirmed Brother Lucius apologetically as he tossed the king of diamonds on the table. "Exceptionally bad luck, Abbot. A most cruel distribution of the cards."

"Wait a minute," cried the Abbot, turning accusingly towards East. "If your last card is a heart, what on earth happened to your queen of clubs?"

But East, seeming not to hear the question, just stroked his beard in a leisurely manner and smiled amiably back at him.

No one seemed very keen to cut in, seeing that Brother Anthony was at the table, so the same four soldiered on well into the night. The kibitzers had long since retired to their cells when the final rubber saw the Abbot in partnership with Brother Anthony.

N–S game, dealer West

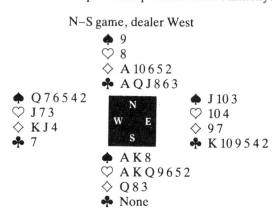

```
                    ♠ 9
                    ♡ 8
                    ◇ A 10 6 5 2
                    ♣ A Q J 8 6 3
  ♠ Q 7 6 5 4 2           N           ♠ J 10 3
  ♡ J 7 3                               ♡ 10 4
  ◇ K J 4          W         E         ◇ 9 7
  ♣ 7                      S            ♣ K 10 9 5 4 2
                    ♠ A K 8
                    ♡ A K Q 9 6 5 2
                    ◇ Q 8 3
                    ♣ None
```

Brother Lucius Defends

S	W	N	E
The	Bro.	Bro.	Bro.
Abbot	Damien	Anthony	Lucius
	No	No	1 ♡
dble	No	No	1 ♠
6 ♡	End		

After two passes Brother Lucius found himself in a familiar tactical situation. North–South could surely chalk up an easy game somewhere, and if he were to pass, the Abbot would doubtless place his partner with some values and bid accordingly. Brother Lucius therefore decided to risk a psychic one-heart opening. The Abbot, struggling unsuccessfully with the wrapping on a new tube of mints, glanced dismissively to his right and made an obvious double.

Hoping to obscure the issue further, Brother Lucius ducked out into one spade. The Abbot expressed his disdain for such frivolities with a bold leap to six hearts. Brother Damien led his singleton club and Brother Anthony spread his minor two-suiter on the table.

"Yes, just what I'd expected," declared the Abbot merrily. "Thank you, partner."

The Abbot tried his luck with the queen of clubs, ruffing when the king appeared. Dummy's top two clubs would now account for the diamond losers so the Abbot proceeded to take a spade ruff to guard against a 4–1 trump break. When he tried to regain entry to hand by trumping a small club with the nine, Brother Damien overruffed and dealt the contract a mortal blow by returning the king of diamonds.

"That was most unlucky, Abbot," commented Brother Damien as he entered a neatly-scribed 100 on his scorepad. "I'm sure I've missed something, but couldn't you just have taken twelve tricks and not bothered about the overtrick?"

"Overtrick?" barked the Abbot. "What in heaven's name are you talking about? I was simply guarding against the trumps being 4–1."

"No, no, trumps were 3–2," replied Brother Damien helpfully. "I had three to the jack. If you draw trumps you do make twelve tricks."

"Yes, thank you very much, I had noticed," growled the Abbot. "My play was well in line with the odds. Even allowing for the lead

[31]

being slightly suspicious, the chance of a club overruff must be less than a 4–1 trump division."

"I'm sure you're right, Abbot," said Brother Lucius. "My bidding in the majors left little room for a six-card club suit."

Ignoring this remark, the Abbot rose to his feet. "Much as I enjoy partnering you, Brother Anthony," he said, "I fear I shall have to cut the rubber short. It's past midnight and I've had a busy day."

6

Sergeant Barker's Aberration

As the Abbot's ancient Austin Seven pulled up at the red and white barrier, an armed sentry approached.

"May I ask your business here, sir?" asked the sentry, peering into the car in what seemed to the Abbot to be an unnecessarily suspicious manner.

"We're here to play a bridge match," replied the Abbot impatiently.

"Yes, sir. I've got two matches down here booked for tonight. Are you Abbot Hugo Yorke-Smith or er ... Dr. Rapanjibat Singh?"

"Dr. Singh till midnight. Then I change back to a pumpkin," retorted the Abbot. "Come on, man, let us through. We're ten minutes late already."

"... back to a pumpkin at midnight," wrote the sentry on his clipboard.

Game all, dealer West

	♠ Q 10 7 5	
	♡ 10 9	
	◇ A 7 4	
	♣ A J 7 4	

♠ 4   ♠ 6
♡ A Q J 8 7   ♡ 6 3 2
◇ 9 8 5   ◇ J 10 6 2
♣ K Q 8 2   ♣ 10 9 6 5 3

♠ A K J 9 8 3 2
♡ K 5 4
◇ K Q 3
♣ None

S	W	N	E
Col.	Bro.	Sgt.	The
Whacket	Lucius	Barker	Abbot
		1 ♡	dble	No
6 ♠	End		

[33]

The splendidly moustached Colonel Whacket, sitting South, was rather surprised to hear his partner produce a vulnerable take-out double. The Colonel's first thought was to apply his favourite convention, Roman Blackwood. If his partner were to show two aces of the same colour, seven spades would be an excellent prospect. However, two good arguments against the bid occurred to him. A one-ace response would not assist him and a five-spade response showing two aces of the same rank would place the contract in the wrong hand. He therefore leapt to six spades and received the lead of the king of clubs.

"Double's a bit underweight, sir," reported Sgt. Barker as he put down the dummy.

The Colonel ruffed the lead, crossed to a trump and ruffed another club. A flurry of trumps and diamond honours left these cards outstanding:

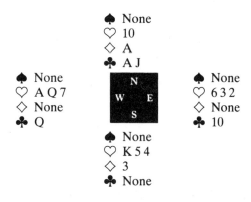

At this point the declarer led a diamond to the ace. For some while it had been clear to Brother Lucius in the West seat that a three-card ending was threatened, and to avoid this he had bared the queen of clubs. On the last diamond he threw a deceptive queen of hearts.

Seeming not to notice East's discard of the club ten, the Colonel gave the underside of his moustache a triumphant lick and threw West in with dummy's ten of hearts. When West unexpectedly produced the seven of hearts, declarer won in hand with the king and conceded the last trick to East's six.

The Abbot was delighted that his miserable hand had somehow

furnished the setting trick. "I had to let the ten of clubs go," he said. "Did you see that, Lucius?"

The Colonel was still puzzled as to how he had gone down.

"Something funny about that," he announced eventually.

"If you'd happened to lead the ace of clubs at the finish, sir, the queen would have fallen," observed Sgt. Barker.

"It's against mess rules to criticise an officer's play!" snapped the Colonel. "If it happens again you'll be on a charge."

Brother Lucius raised his eyebrows at this exchange. For years he had assumed that the Abbot was the most unreasonable partner in the world. Maybe he'd been wrong.

"It was an interesting ending," commented the Abbot, tactless as ever. "The ace of diamonds actually squeezed me in a sense. If I throw the ten of clubs declarer knows the table's clubs are good, and if I throw a heart, and you discard the queen, declarer's last two hearts will be established."

A few boards later Sgt. Barker picked up one of the finest hands he had ever held. Rather unexpectedly it was his partner, Colonel Whacket, who opened the bidding.

N–S game, dealer South

```
              ♠ A K Q 10 6 2
              ♡ A K J 6
              ◇ A K 4
              ♣ Void
  ♠ 9 4                        ♠ J 7 3
  ♡ 7 2          N             ♡ Q 9 8 5 3
  ◇ 10 7 6    W     E          ◇ Q 9 3
  ♣ 9 7 5 4 3 2    S           ♣ 8 6
              ♠ 8 5
              ♡ 10 4
              ◇ J 8 5 2
              ♣ A K Q J 10
```

S	W	N	E
Col.	Bro.	Sgt.	The
Whacket	Lucius	Barker	Abbot
1 ♣	No	2 ♠	No
3 ♣	No	3 ♡	No
3 NT	No	4 ◇	No
4 NT	No	6 NT	End

[35]

When the Colonel showed no inclination to support his spades, Sgt. Barker settled for a small slam in no-trumps. The nine of spades was led and the dummy was laid out in three straight lines as if awaiting kit inspection.

"Not a bad dummy, Sergeant," said the Colonel, spotting a chance to steal an entry to hand. "Play the ten."

The Abbot eyed this card with a good deal of suspicion. Why had declarer given up a perfectly reasonable chance of bringing in the spades for no loser? Divining the Colonel's low plot, the Abbot allowed dummy's ten to win the trick.

Annoyed that his first manoeuvre had been thwarted, the Colonel continued with the knave of hearts. This card also was allowed to hold.

Declarer now cashed his major suit winners, West discarding five clubs, East two clubs and a heart. This was the four-card ending:

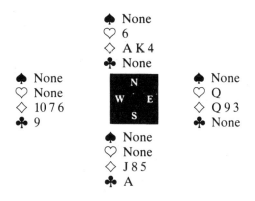

```
                    ♠ None
                    ♡ 6
                    ◇ A K 4
                    ♣ None
    ♠ None                        ♠ None
    ♡ None          N             ♡ Q
    ◇ 10 7 6    W       E         ◇ Q 9 3
    ♣ 9             S             ♣ None
                    ♠ None
                    ♡ None
                    ◇ J 8 5
                    ♣ A
```

Uncertain whether to exit in diamonds or hearts, the Colonel decided to rely on fate.

"When's your wife's birthday, Sergeant?" he asked suddenly. If it was an odd day of the month he would play East for the queen of diamonds.

"Some time in March, I believe, sir," replied Sgt. Barker stolidly.

"Which day, man?" demanded the Colonel.

"16th, sir," said the Sergeant firmly.

"Play the ace of diamonds, then," instructed the Colonel. "And the king . . . and a small diamond."

This proved to be the wrong decision and the slam failed. The

Colonel glowered at his partner, but before he could say anything, the Abbot intervened.

"I imagine Brother Xavier will play it in spades in the other room," he said. "How does that go?"

"Any lead but a trump gives an easy thirteen tricks," replied Brother Lucius. "And a small trump is little better because West has to cover and declarer can enter dummy by ruffing the third round of hearts."

"Yes, it looks as if your East player will need to lead the jack of trumps, Colonel," said the Abbot with a self-satisfied smile. "That's the only lead to topple seven spades. It also beats six spades if the declarer goes for a heart ruff."

"Maybe I was wrong about the wife's birthday," said Sgt. Barker thoughtfully. "It could be the 15th. I'll find out and draft a report for you tomorrow, sir."

7

The Abbot Recuperates

The Abbot was going through an alarmingly bad patch. As a result of overwork and the tail-end of a persistent cold he had been unable to maintain his concentration and was a heavy loser on the week so far.

"See you at the £1 table after supper, Abbot?" asked Brother Lucius hopefully.

"No, I've been neglecting some of our lesser brethren," replied the Abbot piously. "I'm going to pay a social visit to the 5p game."

Love all, dealer South

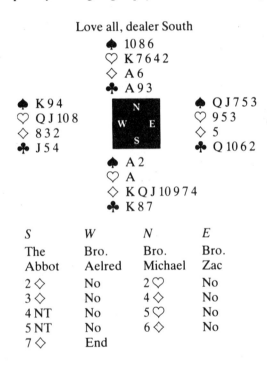

```
              ♠ 10 8 6
              ♡ K 7 6 4 2
              ◇ A 6
              ♣ A 9 3
♠ K 9 4                        ♠ Q J 7 5 3
♡ Q J 10 8         N          ♡ 9 5 3
◇ 8 3 2        W       E      ◇ 5
♣ J 5 4            S          ♣ Q 10 6 2
              ♠ A 2
              ♡ A
              ◇ K Q J 10 9 7 4
              ♣ K 8 7
```

S	W	N	E
The	Bro.	Bro.	Bro.
Abbot	Aelred	Michael	Zac
2 ◇	No	2 ♡	No
3 ◇	No	4 ◇	No
4 NT	No	5 ♡	No
5 NT	No	6 ◇	No
7 ◇	End		

The Abbot was greeted by some rather nervous smiles as he took a seat at one of the 5p tables. On the very first hand he picked up a delightful 17-count, and a crisp interchange of bids landed him in a diamond grand slam. Brother Aelred led the queen of hearts and the Abbot won in hand.

"Just arranging," said the Abbot, as he spread dummy's disappointing heart suit.

The only straightforward chance of making the contract was to ruff the fifth heart good, but dummy appeared to be an entry short for this. The Abbot, like most other monks belonging to the mathematical Archimedean order, was extremely proud of his proficiency at mental arithmetic. In less time than it takes to work out a Blackwood response, he calculated that to drop the eight of trumps singleton was only a 12 per cent shot. A finesse of the dummy's six, to create an extra entry, was therefore considerably more promising.

With this intention he led the four of diamonds; but Brother Aelred followed annoyingly with the eight, forcing dummy's ace and eclipsing all hope of two trump entries to the table. Just what's been happening to me all week, thought the Abbot bitterly. Forced to rely on the rather unlikely club–heart squeeze or some other miracle, the Abbot grumpily ruffed a low heart and reeled off three more rounds of trumps, discovering that West's eight of diamonds was not even a singleton. The following cards remained:

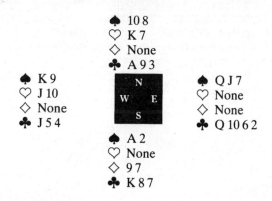

On the penultimate trump Brother Aelred, sitting West, discarded a club while North and East both threw spades. Feeling that something interesting was brewing up and hoping to give the impression that he knew exactly what it was, the Abbot led out his last trump. All three hands released a club and when the Abbot now played off the king and ace of clubs, West had to bare his spade king to keep the hearts guarded. Similarly, when the king of hearts followed, East had to bare the spade queen. The Abbot finally crossed back to the ace of spades and was delighted to find that the two of spades, initially the least promising card in his hand, had become a triumphant winner.

"Superbly played, Abbot," said Brother Aelred. "We don't usually see this sort of play in our game."

"Well, I must say you played well by inserting the eight of diamonds," replied the Abbot. "Perhaps you were watching when I defended a similar hand last week?"

"I'm not sure about that, Abbot," replied Brother Aelred, somewhat confused. "I saw the play in a book actually, I believe it's called a trump echo. I could have played the three, of course, but I thought partner might read it as my lowest."

"What type of squeeze was it, Abbot?" enquired Brother Michael.

"Er . . . well, it was er . . . have you read *De Constrictibus Multis*; Cardinal Perazzini's ten-volume masterwork on squeezes?"

"Not recently, Abbot," replied Brother Michael carefully.

"Well, according to his classification it was a translateral squeeze, type VIIIb, with duplicated menaces."

"Good gracious, Abbot. That sounds impressive," said Brother Aelred. "It certainly makes my trump echo look a bit tame. I must say, we do appreciate you joining our little game."

The Abbot gazed wistfully across the cardroom to where a lively £1 game was in progress.

"I feel it's my duty to give equal attention to all my flock," he replied. "Now, whose deal is it?"

8

Brother Aelred Regrets

"How in heaven's name did you make four spades on board 13?" demanded the Abbot when Brother Xavier arrived at his table. "I had to play it well to get out for one down."

"Oh, that was against Brother Aelred," smiled Brother Xavier. "He led the jack of . . ."

"Spare me the gory details," interrupted the Abbot. "Anything can happen against Brother Aelred. Now, let's proceed. You dealt."

E–W game, dealer South

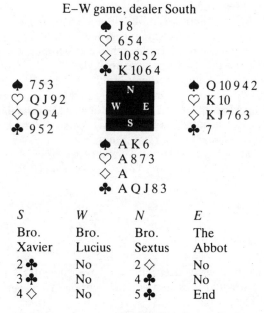

```
              ♠ J 8
              ♡ 6 5 4
              ◇ 10 8 5 2
              ♣ K 10 6 4
♠ 7 5 3                        ♠ Q 10 9 4 2
♡ Q J 9 2          N          ♡ K 10
◇ Q 9 4        W     E        ◇ K J 7 6 3
♣ 9 5 2            S          ♣ 7
              ♠ A K 6
              ♡ A 8 7 3
              ◇ A
              ♣ A Q J 8 3
```

S	W	N	E
Bro.	Bro.	Bro.	The
Xavier	Lucius	Sextus	Abbot
2 ♣	No	2 ◇	No
3 ♣	No	4 ♣	No
4 ◇	No	5 ♣	End

Brother Lucius led a trump against five clubs and declarer won in hand. As he might want to ruff the fourth round of hearts, his first play was a small heart from hand. Brother Lucius went in with the knave, to make sure of winning the trick, and fired back another trump. The king won in dummy and the Abbot, to avoid winning the next heart trick, discarded the king of hearts.

Declarer now played a heart to the ace, discovering that the defenders' last trump was in the same hand as the remaining hearts. Undeterred, he went boldly for his last chance, a low spade to the knave. When East produced the queen, declarer was home. He discarded a heart on the top spades and ruffed two hearts on the table.

"A brilliant defensive effort gone to waste," complained the Abbot as he just beat North to the scoresheet. "Yes, I thought so. One 630, five 600s and some idiot pair one down in the slam. Dead average."

"That's funny," said Brother Xavier. "Do I really just get an average? I thought I played it rather well."

"Perhaps your unblock of the heart king wasn't such a good idea after all, Abbot," commented Brother Lucius. "It pushed declarer into the winning line."

The Abbot felt there was probably some flaw in this observation but hesitated to risk an argument. A few boards later he spotted Brother Aelred approaching his table and whispered urgently to Brother Lucius that two tops were needed.

"How are you doing, Brother Aelred?" he asked in a bluff tone.

"Not badly at all," said Brother Aelred. "My partner made a fine slam a little while ago. I don't think we shall be bottom this time."

The Abbot consulted his hand. "One diamond," he announced aggressively, hoping to deter any intervention.

"Er . . . no bid," said Brother Michael respectfully.

Brother Lucius, the Abbot's partner, gazed at an 11-count full of potential:

♠ 3
♡ 9 4 3
♢ K Q 7 2
♣ A Q 10 8 3

Very likely a close decision would be called for later in the auction, particularly as it was pairs scoring. However, the first response was automatic.

"One heart," he declared. Whatever the final denomination, the first essential was to deflect a heart lead.

"One spade," ventured Brother Aelred.

"Four hearts," bellowed the Abbot.

"Four spades," said Brother Michael bravely.

Brother Lucius fingered his 11-count in some concern. There

were excellent prospects of twelve tricks in diamonds, but if he bid six diamonds straightaway the Abbot was all too likely to revert to the higher scoring heart slam. Brother Lucius spotted a way to get his message across.

"Five diamonds," he announced – a deliberate underbid.

"Five hearts," replied the Abbot, as expected.

"Six diamonds," said Brother Lucius, well satisfied with his chosen sequence. Surely even the Abbot would not be so wooden as to misinterpret the situation.

"Six hearts," said the Abbot, looking puzzled.

With the air of a saint Brother Lucius passed and waited for the appearance of dummy's trump suit. His heart sank as the Abbot's trump support hit the table – a moth-eaten K 10 x x.

N–S game, dealer North

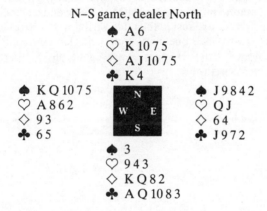

```
                    ♠ A 6
                    ♡ K 10 7 5
                    ◇ A J 10 7 5
                    ♣ K 4
  ♠ K Q 10 7 5          N          ♠ J 9 8 4 2
  ♡ A 8 6 2        W        E      ♡ Q J
  ◇ 9 3                 S          ◇ 6 4
  ♣ 6 5                            ♣ J 9 7 2
                    ♠ 3
                    ♡ 9 4 3
                    ◇ K Q 8 2
                    ♣ A Q 10 8 3
```

The bidding had been:

S	W	N	E
Bro.	Bro.	The	Bro.
Lucius	Aelred	Abbot	Michael
		1 ◇	No
1 ♡	1 ♠	4 ♡	4 ♠
5 ◇	No	5 ♡	No
6 ◇	No	6 ♡	End

Brother Lucius captured the spade lead in dummy. The slam seemed dead from the start, and prospects of reviving it about as hopeless as giving a skeleton the kiss of life. Perhaps if West had a doubleton club he could be tempted to ruff in front of dummy . . . Playing for this chance, Brother Lucius led the king of clubs and successfully finessed the ten. He then led the ace of clubs and reached towards dummy's spade.

"Having none?" said Brother Michael as Brother Aelred pounced on the club ace with a trump.

Looking as annoyed as he could without actually being unethical, Brother Lucius overruffed and returned to hand with a diamond. The queen of clubs followed.

"Having none?" said East again as Brother Aelred ruffed in for a second time.

"No, I still can't find any," replied Brother Aelred happily, delighted at being able to thwart his formidable opponent.

Brother Lucius overruffed again and returned to hand with another diamond honour. A trump to the king and a trump back to the queen and ace exhausted the table's trumps, but Brother Lucius was able to ruff West's queen of spades and claim the contract.

"Well done!" cried Brother Aelred generously. "Partner, we ought to have sacrificed."

9

The Miracle on the 5p Table

Brother Aelred closed the heavy oak door of his cell and threw himself dejectedly on the narrow bed. It wasn't losing he minded so much, it was . . . well, the *attitude* of the other players.

The level of politeness at the 5p tables frequented by Brother Aelred was far superior to that at the £1 table, where the Abbot himself set the standard. However, the brave smiles when his colleagues cut him as partner and the strained silences that followed his attempts at dummy play were as wounding as outright criticism. As he contemplated the ceiling of his cell, a bold idea came to him.

That night at 2 a.m., clutching a candlestick in one hand and a Latin dictionary in the other, Brother Aelred crept silently up the stone stairway to the monastery library. Shivering with cold, he pulled down a heavy leather-bound tome from the top shelf. It was volume VII of Cardinal Perazzini's life-work on squeeze-play, *De Constrictibus Multis*.

Written in Church Latin with the hand diagrams inscribed in Roman numerals and the four players represented by effigies of the saints, it was not the most readable of works. Nevertheless it was widely regarded as a scholarly masterpiece, compiled in the late eighteenth century when whist players in Britain were struggling with such simplicities as the Bath Coup.

Opening the huge book randomly, at page 672, Brother Aelred began to scribble out a translation of the analysis of a particularly complex hand.

"Cordium decem transfixo victor sex versus est . . ." he murmured, flicking busily through his dictionary. "Ah yes, ablative absolute . . . The ten of hearts having been pinned, the six became a winner."

Soon his clandestine task was completed. He returned the book to its resting place on the top shelf and tiptoed back to his cell, where he spent the next few minutes preparing a pack of cards.

The following afternoon Brother Aelred walked purposefully into the cardroom and joined in one of the 5p games. After a few hands it was his turn to deal.

"Goodness me!" exclaimed Brother Aelred. "Who's that cleaning the windows over there? It's not the Abbot, is it?"

Three pairs of eyes darted across the room, and Brother Aelred smoothly switched packs under the table.

"No, of course not," chuckled Brother Zac, "unless he's lost three or four stone overnight and had his hair cut as well. No, I think it's Brother Rupert."

Brother Aelred proceeded to deal the following layout, the very one that he had studied at such length the previous night.

N–S game, dealer South

Brother Aelred passed on the South cards and, as expected, his partner opened two clubs. The auction now had to be manoeuvred in the direction of a spade grand slam.

"Two spades," replied Brother Aelred.

"Two no-trumps," came the rebid from Brother Zac.

"Three spades," persisted Brother Aelred. Now if his partner cue-bid in clubs, he could bid four diamonds and they would be well on the way towards the grand.

"Three no-trumps," said Brother Zac.

What an excruciatingly selfish effort, thought Brother Aelred, glaring reproachfully across the table. Surely even a 5p player could visualise a spade slam with all those controls facing a positive response and a rebid spade suit. It was clear to Brother Aelred that he would have to take charge of the auction himself.

"Four no-trumps?" he bid, with the special intonation that accompanies a Blackwood enquiry.

"Six no-trumps," replied Brother Zac woodenly.

"Seven spades," declared Brother Aelred, closing his fan. "It's your lead, Brother Michael."

"The bidding is not yet over," said Brother Zac reprovingly.

Brother Aelred realised to his horror that his partner was counting the score. Doubtless he was determining whether the extra ten points for 7 NT would bring in an additional 5p.

"I thought the Abbot's recent sermon on cupidity was particularly forceful, didn't you?" he asked of the table at large.

"Makes no difference," said Brother Zac after a recount. "I pass."

The knave of hearts was led and Brother Zac displayed his handsome dummy.

"Oh. Not quite what I'd expected," said Brother Aelred untruthfully. "Still, never mind. I'll see what I can do."

He paused for a while, appearing to plan the play. In reality his mind had begun to flood with last minute doubts about the whole venture. What if the deal were recognised and his misdemeanour discovered? He could invoke coincidence, but . . .

"Are you feeling all right, Brother Aelred?"

"Of course. A hand like this calls for detailed planning, that's all."

As recommended by Cardinal Perazzini, Brother Aelred played the ace of hearts and two rounds of trumps, followed by the three top diamonds and a trump to hand. The end position detailed on page 673 of volume VII had now been reached:

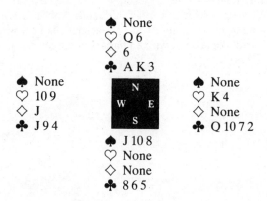

When the knave of spades was led, West was already in trouble. A diamond discard would establish dummy's six, a heart discard would allow his other heart to be pinned by dummy's queen and if he gave up his club guard his partner would become exposed to a trump squeeze.

"What's the contract, Brother Aelred?" boomed an unmistakable voice suddenly.

Brother Aelred's stomach almost leapt on to the table. The Abbot! What was he doing here?

"It's er ... seven spades actually, Abbot," replied Brother Aelred, beginning to wish the whole wretched idea had never occurred to him.

"Hmm. Most interesting. Well, don't let me interrupt you. Carry on playing."

West threw a club, and so did both the dummy and East. Brother Aelred judged that, even with the Abbot standing at his shoulder, he had nothing to lose by following the prescribed line of play. He therefore continued with another trump from hand, discarding the six of diamonds from dummy. East released his small heart, hoping for the best. Swallowing hard, Brother Aelred crossed to the club ace and ruffed out East's king of hearts, establishing dummy's queen as his thirteenth trick.

"Brother Aelred has just performed a triple pinning squeeze on West followed by a ruffing squeeze on East," announced the Abbot dramatically. "The day of miracles is not done. I shall bring this to the notice of the appropriate College of Cardinals. His Holiness himself should be informed."

"The moment I started to play the hand, Abbot, a remarkable feeling came over me," said Brother Aelred. "I felt ... inspired."

"Aah," said the Abbot, with an understanding nod.

10

The Abbot Makes a Proposal

"One of the most intolerant regimes I have ever come across," muttered the Abbot, who had an open letter in his hand.

"Who's that, Abbot?" enquired Brother Lucius.

"The English Bridge Union. They have rejected my application to make the national inter-monastery championship a green point event. They also refuse to accept an all-male team for the Hubert Phillips Bowl, making no allowance for our predicament. I had thought to meet the case by including one of the lay choristers. That new boy, Adrian."

"I have an aged cousin who used to play regularly," said Brother Lucius. "She belongs to a Carmelite Order not far from Winchester. Perhaps, in the interests of Church unity, her Order might grant her a dispensation to play in our team."

"I suppose it's worth a try," replied the Abbot, scratching his ear dubiously. "On average she'll cost us 100 points a board, I dare say. Well, the rest of us will have to pull that back."

The negotiations were completed and in the first round the monastery team was drawn at home against a team of university dons. As it was out of the question to allow a female to invade the precincts of the monastery for the first time since its foundation in the early sixteenth century, the match was played at the local Dolphin Hotel.

At the Monastery of St. Titus

Board 4.   Game all, dealer West

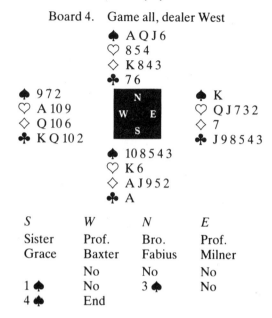

```
              ♠ A Q J 6
              ♡ 8 5 4
              ◇ K 8 4 3
              ♣ 7 6
♠ 9 7 2                        ♠ K
♡ A 10 9          N           ♡ Q J 7 3 2
◇ Q 10 6       W     E        ◇ 7
♣ K Q 10 2        S           ♣ J 9 8 5 4 3
              ♠ 10 8 5 4 3
              ♡ K 6
              ◇ A J 9 5 2
              ♣ A
```

S	W	N	E
Sister	Prof.	Bro.	Prof.
Grace	Baxter	Fabius	Milner
	No	No	No
1 ♠	No	3 ♠	No
4 ♠	End		

After some academic reflection Professor Baxter pulled out the king of clubs as his opening lead. Sister Grace won in hand, played a spade to the ace, dropping the singleton king, and then drew two more rounds of trumps.

Good gracious, thought Brother Fabius in alarm, she doesn't even know about finessing. What an incredible stroke of luck, dropping a singleton king. Unless . . . no, surely not. Though some of these old girls can be pretty unscrupulous.

Sister Grace proceeded to ruff the last club and then play king, ace and another diamond, endplaying West for an overtrick.

"Well played, Sister," said Brother Fabius in a firm tone. "A remarkable example of feminine intuition, don't you agree, Professor?"

"Er . . . yes. Yes, indeed," replied Professor Milner, edging his chair backwards.

"If you are referring to my play in the trump suit," said Sister Grace, "surely it's clear that I must, if possible, avert a lead through my king of hearts. To finesse would be a clear mistake."

"Quite so," said Professor Baxter, smiling at his partner.

"In any case, it must be a flat board," declared Sister Grace. "Your other pair could hardly miss such an elementary safety play."

Board 10.   Game all, dealer North

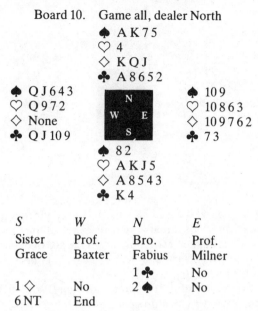

♠ A K 7 5
♡ 4
◇ K Q J
♣ A 8 6 5 2

♠ Q J 6 4 3
♡ Q 9 7 2
◇ None
♣ Q J 10 9

♠ 10 9
♡ 10 8 6 3
◇ 10 9 7 6 2
♣ 7 3

♠ 8 2
♡ A K J 5
◇ A 8 5 4 3
♣ K 4

S	W	N	E
Sister	Prof.	Bro.	Prof.
Grace	Baxter	Fabius	Milner
		1 ♣	No
1 ◇	No	2 ♠	No
6 NT	End		

Back at the convent Sister Grace would have chosen a more scientific sequence, but she had no great regard for the monks' bidding and wanted to protect them from any difficult decisions.

West led the queen of clubs, which Sister Grace ducked. On the surface there were eleven top tricks with several chances for a twelfth. But when declarer won the second club and started on the diamonds, West showed out. His first three discards were two spades and a heart. The ace of clubs followed, East and South both discarding spades.

From West's discards it seemed likely that he had started with 5–4–0–4 distribution. The crucial question was which defender held the queen of hearts. On the slender evidence that West might have spared more than one discard from a suit at best ten-high, Sister Grace decided to play West for the queen of hearts. Spurning the finesse, she crossed back to hand with the ace of hearts, arriving at the end position overleaf:

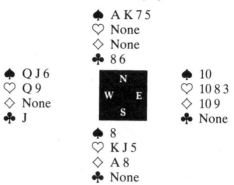

♠ A K 7 5
♡ None
♢ None
♣ 8 6

♠ Q J 6
♡ Q 9
♢ None
♣ J

♠ 10
♡ 10 8 3
♢ 10 9
♣ None

♠ 8
♡ K J 5
♢ A 8
♣ None

Sister Grace began to draw out the king of hearts, but just in time she pushed it back. Two tricks would be needed from the squeeze and none of dummy's threats could be spared at this point.

Revising her plan, declarer laid down the ace of diamonds. West could only throw a heart, and the two heart honours squeezed him again for the twelfth trick.

"Yes, that was painful," declared Professor Baxter, as he marked up his scorecard with an old-fashioned red fountain-pen. "Are you one off if I lead a spade?"

"Gracious, no," replied Sister Grace, adjusting her spectacles. "I can't duck a club, it's true, but I unblock the diamonds, cross to the king of clubs and play the ace of diamonds. You're squeezed without the count, the hand plays itself."

Looking across the table she noticed that Brother Fabius had his mouth open and was looking stunned.

"Chin up, Brother Fabius," she said. "We made the slam, didn't we? Your bidding gave me an excellent picture of your hand."

At the other table the bidding was more orthodox:

S	W	N	E
Prof.	Bro.	Mrs.	The
Carter	Lucius	Milner	Abbot
		1 ♣	No
1 ♢	No	1 ♠	No
2 ♡	No	4 ♢	No
6 ♢	End		

Brother Lucius led the queen of clubs and Professor Carter won in hand. When West showed out on the first round of trumps, the professor showed no sign of annoyance. His eyes gleamed at the intellectual challenge this presented.

After some thought he cashed all the side-suit ace-kings and led a spade from dummy in this end position:

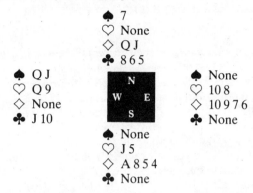

```
                    ♠ 7
                    ♡ None
                    ◇ Q J
                    ♣ 8 6 5
  ♠ Q J                             ♠ None
  ♡ Q 9          ┌─────────┐        ♡ 10 8
  ◇ None         │   N     │        ◇ 10 9 7 6
  ♣ J 10         │ W   E   │        ♣ None
                 │   S     │
                 └─────────┘
                    ♠ None
                    ♡ J 5
                    ◇ A 8 5 4
                    ♣ None
```

The Abbot found the best defence by ruffing with the diamond ten. When the professor countered by discarding a heart from hand, the Abbot gave a resigned nod of the head. Eventually he returned a trump, but declarer could now ruff a club, ruff his last heart and then lead a club from dummy towards his ace-eight of trumps.

The Abbot was in one of his blackest moods as he returned to compare scores at the end of the first ten boards.

"A hopeless set," he announced despondently. "We were given nothing at all. They made five games, two of them thin ones. Brother Lucius got caught in one no-trump doubled on board 2, and they made a vulnerable slam on board 10."

"Sounds fairly flat," said Brother Fabius casually, watching the Abbot's reaction with immense enjoyment. "What happened on board 4?"

"Board 4?" replied the Abbot gruffly. "That was an automatic one down, wasn't it? We took the king of trumps, two hearts and a diamond."

"Really?" exclaimed Brother Fabius. "Sister Grace made an overtrick in our room."

With the monastery team in the lead by 520 aggregate, partnerships were switched in accordance with the rules of the event.

As Brother Fabius and Brother Lucius left the room for the second set, the Abbot looked across at the upright figure of Sister Grace with a new-found respect. Catching her attention, he leaned forward in a confidential manner.

"Have you ever thought of playing in the Cheltenham Mixed Pairs?" he whispered hopefully.

11

The Abbot and the Coffee Jug

"I see the Abbot's team won their Hubert Phillips match last night,"
said Brother Sextus, reaching for the marmalade.

"How do you know that?" asked Brother Aelred, giving his
boiled egg a rather timid tap.

"Well, he's never normally down to breakfast this early," replied
Brother Sextus. "In fact if he loses a match he often has breakfast in
his cell. Look out, he's coming this way."

"Ah! May I join you?" boomed a loud voice. "We had an
interesting hand in our match last night."

The Abbot placed his heavily-laden breakfast tray on the oak
table, sat down and began to scribble out two hands.

"Here, bid these two. There's some intervention coming."

```
♠ A Q 9 6 2            ♠ 5
♡ 7 4                  ♡ A 10 6 3
♦ K 9                  ♦ Q 8
♣ K 10 8 2             ♣ A Q J 9 6 4
```

"It's you to bid first, Brother Sextus," mumbled the Abbot, who
had already started on his egg and bacon.

"One spade," said Brother Sextus.

"Two clubs," ventured Brother Aelred.

"Right," said the Abbot. "Now the next hand comes in with two
hearts."

Brother Sextus rebid three clubs and Brother Aelred, uncertain
whether three hearts would show a heart stop or ask for one, bid
three hearts anyway. Brother Sextus, who was not sure either,
played safe with a simple bid of four clubs, which was raised to five.

"Yes, a somewhat conservative auction, I must say," commented
the Abbot. "Anyhow it's a play hand really. The lead is the king of
hearts and we were in six clubs. How do you play it?"

"This was never a three-minute egg," replied Brother Aelred,
seeking to introduce a diversion. "Look at it. It's almost hard-
boiled."

"Well, you certainly need the spade finesse," said Brother
Sextus, inspecting the diagram with a frown, "and spades 4–3 as

well. Then you can discard both your diamonds and eventually ruff a couple of hearts."

"Yes, but you can't manage all that if the trumps are 3–0," said the Abbot. "Look, I'll put in the other two hands and tell you what happened."

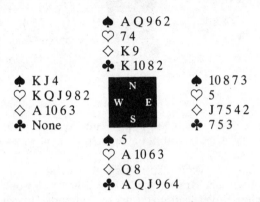

"I won the heart lead and finessed the spade queen," continued the Abbot. "Then I threw a diamond on the ace of spades and ruffed a spade high . . ."

"Er . . . excuse me, Abbot," interrupted Brother Aelred. "Is there any coffee left in that jug?"

". . . then I played a trump to the king, exposing the break, and ruffed the last spade good."

"Would you mind passing the coffee?" persisted Brother Aelred.

"Can't you wait till I've finished the hand?" exclaimed the Abbot heatedly. "There's a most interesting end position coming up. Now, where was I?"

"You'd just ruffed the last spade good," replied Brother Sextus.

"Ah yes. Well, now I had to draw trumps before I could throw my last diamond on the long spade, and that left me with only one trump to deal with two losing hearts."

"Very unlucky," said Brother Sextus. "Still, it was a most interesting hand, Abbot. One of the most interesting that I've . . ."

"Don't be absurd," grunted the Abbot. "I haven't finished telling you what happened yet. On the last spade West had to reduce himself to two hearts to keep the ace of diamonds guarded. I'll write down the end position:

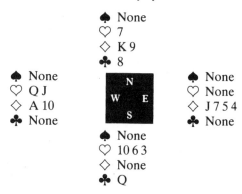

♠ None
♡ 7
♢ K 9
♣ 8

♠ None
♡ Q J
♢ A 10
♣ None

♠ None
♡ None
♢ J 7 5 4
♣ None

♠ None
♡ 10 6 3
♢ None
♣ Q

"As you can see, I was now able to endplay West with a heart," concluded the Abbot, celebrating his achievement with a forkload of bacon.

"I still think we were right to stop in five clubs," said Brother Aelred with an uncharacteristic lack of tact. "You wouldn't have made six clubs if West had led the ace of diamonds. How did you get so high?"

The Abbot rose to his feet. "The lesson of the hand lies in my handling of the dummy," he said blackly. "If you had paid a little more attention you might have learnt something for a change. I must be off now. A good day to you both."

"I say, you were a bit bold there," said Brother Sextus, his disapproval tempered with admiration. "I'm always rather careful what I say to the Abbot."

"So am I usually," replied Brother Aelred. "But it really annoyed me when he wouldn't pass the coffee. Can I pour you another cup?"

12

Brother Xavier's Recall

It was a typical afternoon for the time of year and a bitterly cold wind was sweeping round the monastery grounds. Inside the cardroom warmth prevailed, thanks to a splendid log fire, and several fours were in progress.

"One no-trump," said Brother Xavier, eyeing his 16-count contentedly. Surely there was no better way of seeing off such a wicked afternoon, he thought, than sitting in the warm, waging battle over the card table.

"No bid," muttered the next player.

"Brother Xavier!" boomed an unmistakable voice. "What are you doing here?"

"Oh, er . . . just having a quick rubber, Abbot."

"When I tell you to weed the monastery front drive I don't mean you should run a mower up and down it for a couple of minutes and then head for the cardroom."

"Yes, I know, but it's freezing out there, Abbot, and I thought . . ."

"Nonsense! Give me your hand and I'll finish the rubber for you," said the Abbot, easing his bulk into the empty chair. "You'll find a trowel in my garage, near the box of empty wine bottles. Now, what's the bidding so far?"

E–W game, dealer North

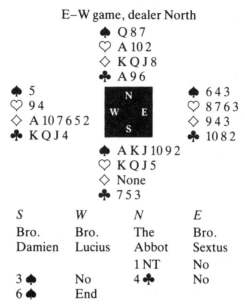

```
              ♠ Q 8 7
              ♡ A 10 2
              ◇ K Q J 8
              ♣ A 9 6
♠ 5                            ♠ 6 4 3
♡ 9 4            N             ♡ 8 7 6 3
◇ A 10 7 6 5 2   W   E         ◇ 9 4 3
♣ K Q J 4           S          ♣ 10 8 2
              ♠ A K J 10 9 2
              ♡ K Q J 5
              ◇ None
              ♣ 7 5 3
```

S	W	N	E
Bro.	Bro.	The	Bro.
Damien	Lucius	Abbot	Sextus
		1 NT	No
3 ♠	No	4 ♣	No
6 ♠	End		

Brother Damien, sitting South, was too overawed by the Abbot's presence to investigate a grand slam. Settling instead for an early jump to six spades, he won the king of clubs lead in dummy and noted with alarm that even six spades was no laydown. When the king of diamonds brought only an unconcerned three from East, Brother Damien decided that the ace was offside and ruffed in hand.

He saw that if trumps were 2–2 he could discard a club from dummy on the fourth heart and ruff a club. There seemed no better plan available, so he cashed the ace and king of trumps; but this manoeuvre also failed to bring any good news, West showing out on the second round. Brother Damien's spirits revived somewhat when East had to follow to four rounds of hearts, permitting a club to be thrown from the dummy. He now exited hopefully with a club towards the nine, but Brother Lucius played the four, allowing his partner to win the trick and return a third round of trumps. Declarer was left with an unavoidable club loser and the slam failed by one trick.

"I'm very sorry, Abbot," said Brother Damien. "Perhaps I should have taken only one round of trumps before running the hearts?"

[58]

"Yes, as the cards lie. But if trumps were 2–2 West would ruff the third heart," replied the Abbot, looking rather irritated. "You must duck the opening lead. Then you can take two rounds of trumps and play out the hearts. That caters for both distributions."

"Are you sure that's the best line, Abbot?" enquired Brother Lucius. "With so many entries to dummy, isn't it possible to play ace of clubs, diamond ruff, heart to the ten, diamond ruff, heart to the ace, diamond ruff, and so on, a complete dummy reversal? If I'm right, this wins unless spades are 4–0 or hearts 5–1."

"Perhaps," said the Abbot after a pause. "You or I would have played it that way. But young players must follow first principles. At this stage a duck of the club ace is all that could be expected of a postulant."

A few hands later Brother Lucius had a chance to end the rubber.

N–S game, dealer West

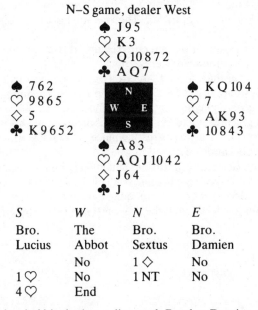

	♠ J 9 5	
	♡ K 3	
	◇ Q 10 8 7 2	
	♣ A Q 7	

♠ 7 6 2		♠ K Q 10 4
♡ 9 8 6 5		♡ 7
◇ 5		◇ A K 9 3
♣ K 9 6 5 2		♣ 10 8 4 3

	♠ A 8 3	
	♡ A Q J 10 4 2	
	◇ J 6 4	
	♣ J	

S	W	N	E
Bro.	The	Bro.	Bro.
Lucius	Abbot	Sextus	Damien
	No	1 ◇	No
1 ♡	No	1 NT	No
4 ♡	End		

The Abbot led his singleton diamond. Brother Damien won with the king, cashed the ace of diamonds and returned the nine, a suit-preference signal directing attention to his handsome spade holding.

The Abbot ruffed and duly returned the seven of spades, but now declarer was home. After drawing trumps he simply crossed to the ace of clubs and discard his two spade losers on the diamonds.

"To tell the truth," remarked Brother Lucius as he totted up the rubber, "I was afraid of a club return after the ruff."

The Abbot thought about this.

"Of course. Why on earth did you ask for a spade return, partner?" he barked, glaring fiercely across the table at Brother Damien. "Surely declarer was marked with six good hearts and the ace of spades?"

"Yes, I suppose so," agreed Brother Damien nervously.

"Then our only chance was that he had a singleton club and could be cut off from the table's diamonds. You should have signalled for a club switch not a spade."

"Yes, of course," gulped Brother Damien. "I'm terribly sorry, Abbot."

"For that matter," the Abbot went on, "you could have returned the nine of diamonds at trick 2. Then we still have everything under control."

"I make the rubber seventeen," remarked Brother Lucius.

"Correct," agreed Brother Sextus.

"As much as that, was it?" queried the Abbot, extracting a purse from somewhere inside his cassock. "5p stakes, I assume."

"No, we were playing for 50p actually."

"Good gracious!" exclaimed the Abbot, snapping his purse shut and returning it firmly to its resting place. "I'm not settling Brother Xavier's debts at those prices."

He strode across the cardroom and flung open the ancient leaded window. It was raining quite hard outside now, but at the end of the monastery drive a miserable kneeling figure could just be seen.

"Brother Xavier!" cried the Abbot. "You're wanted here."

13

Mrs. Bungle's Signal

Brother Lucius eased himself back into the red leather armchair. "Double!" he said, glaring round the table with a singularly fierce expression.

"What on earth are you doing?" asked the Abbot, entering the room suddenly and closing the door behind him.

"Oh er ... hullo, Abbot," replied an embarrassed Brother Lucius. "I was just testing out the seats with a few bids before the match starts."

"Oh, yes," said the Abbot, rather admiring Brother Lucius's thoroughness. "And what conclusions did you come to?"

"Well, whoever sits here will get the sun in his eyes later on, particularly if we pull the curtains right back; and that green chair there is fiendishly uncomfortable. It's got a large spring loose right in the middle."

"Right, I'll just swap these two chairs round then," replied the Abbot, moving with unusual swiftness. "You and I can sit in this direction."

A few seconds later Mr. and Mrs. Bungle arrived and the match began.

N–S game, dealer South

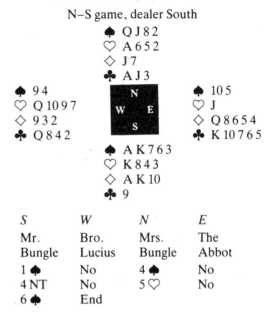

```
                  ♠ Q J 8 2
                  ♡ A 6 5 2
                  ◇ J 7
                  ♣ A J 3
♠ 9 4                               ♠ 10 5
♡ Q 10 9 7          N               ♡ J
◇ 9 3 2         W       E           ◇ Q 8 6 5 4
♣ Q 8 4 2          S                ♣ K 10 7 6 5
                  ♠ A K 7 6 3
                  ♡ K 8 4 3
                  ◇ A K 10
                  ♣ 9
```

S	W	N	E
Mr.	Bro.	Mrs.	The
Bungle	Lucius	Bungle	Abbot
1 ♠	No	4 ♠	No
4 NT	No	5 ♡	No
6 ♠	End		

Mr. Bungle won the trump lead with the ace and drew a second round with the queen. Nervously adjusting his velvet bow-tie, he led the knave of diamonds from dummy. The Abbot, sitting East, naturally played low, and Mr. Bungle put on the ace and eliminated both minor suits, ending in hand. He then led a low heart from hand, intending to duck the trick. This would give him various chances of endplaying one or other defender even if hearts were 4–1.

Seemingly without thought Brother Lucius tossed in a deadly queen of hearts and the slam was one down.

"Yes, you defended well," said Mr. Bungle, screwing up his eyes against the bright sunlight that was now invading the room.

"Well, partner was counted for a singleton," replied Brother Lucius, "and unless it was the knave a first round duck by you was bound to endplay us."

"Yes, yes. Your play of the queen was automatic," butted in the Abbot crossly. "When Mr. Bumble complimented our defence he was presumably referring to my earlier play of withholding the queen of diamonds."

"My name is Bungle actually," came the reply.

"Yes, and appropriately so on this occasion," interjected Mrs. Bungle sharply. "Why didn't you test the hearts first and then fall back on the diamond finesse if necessary? That would be 68 per cent plus half of the remaining 32 per cent, that's er . . . an 86 per cent line."

"My play seemed much the best prospect at the table," replied Mr. Bungle defiantly. "It left the elimination chances intact. Anyway your line was 84 per cent, not 86 per cent."

"My line was plus 1430," declared Mrs. Bungle, shuffling awkwardly in her seat as if trying to find a more comfortable position. "That's the important figure. Yours was minus 100."

When the opponents showed no sign of prolonging their exchange, the Abbot proceeded to deal the next hand.

Love all, dealer South

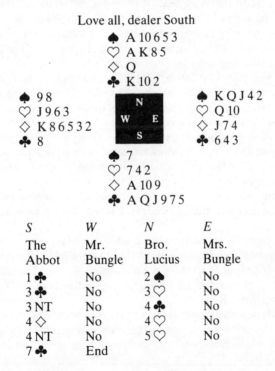

♠ A 10 6 5 3
♡ A K 8 5
♢ Q
♣ K 10 2

♠ 9 8　　　　　　　　　♠ K Q J 4 2
♡ J 9 6 3　　　　　　　♡ Q 10
♢ K 8 6 5 3 2　　　　　♢ J 7 4
♣ 8　　　　　　　　　　♣ 6 4 3

♠ 7
♡ 7 4 2
♢ A 10 9
♣ A Q J 9 7 5

S	W	N	E
The	Mr.	Bro.	Mrs.
Abbot	Bungle	Lucius	Bungle
1 ♣	No	2 ♠	No
3 ♣	No	3 ♡	No
3 NT	No	4 ♣	No
4 ♢	No	4 ♡	No
4 NT	No	5 ♡	No
7 ♣	End		

Having pressed the auction's starter button with a mere 11-count, the Abbot subsequently applied the brakes and suggested stopping in three no-trumps. When his partner showed a club fit, however, the lights changed very much to green and the Abbot accelerated towards the grand slam.

Mr. Bungle considered leading his singleton trump, but rejected it. What would Marguerite say if it trapped her Q x x? He had no wish to find out. Instead he led the nine of spades. The Abbot won in dummy, Mrs. Bungle permitting herself a mild peter of the four to signal her approval of the lead.

The Abbot surveyed the dummy. His diamond losers could be ruffed, and if the spades broke 4–3 the fifth spade could be established. However, the lead of dummy's first suit had an ominous ring about it.

The Abbot crossed to his ace of diamonds and ruffed a diamond. The ten of spades was now covered and ruffed, felling the eight from Mr. Bungle in the West seat. Ruffing his last diamond the Abbot cashed the king of trumps and led the six of spades from dummy. Mrs. Bungle, who had realised to her horror that the dummy's three of spades would become good if she kept on covering, fumbled noticeably before contributing the two.

The Abbot paused for thought. He could ruff the trick high and play for a trump squeeze, which might work if East held four hearts and four spades. The alternative was to run the six of spades, hoping that West held no more trumps.

The Abbot turned to inspect Mrs. Bungle. She certainly was shifting most uncomfortably in her seat, even allowing for the loose spring. Perhaps she had realised that her four of spades at trick one had been misguided.

Taking a deep breath, the Abbot discarded a heart on the six of spades and gave a triumphant grunt when West proved unable to ruff.

"Oh dear, he shouldn't have made that, Marguerite," said Mr. Bungle, shading his eyes so that he could glare across the table at his wife. "Your four of spades gave it to him."

"Don't be so foolish, Edgar," replied his wife. "I had to encourage with K Q J x x."

Mr. Bungle shrugged his shoulders. Such logic was unassailable.

"I realised there was some danger attached to it," persisted Mrs. Bungle, "but if I don't play signals you never know what's happening."

"You're quite right, my dear," said Mr. Bungle. "It was entirely my fault."

14

The Abbot's Raiding Party

Raindrops were in the air as Brother Fabius hastened across the starlit quadrangle. He climbed the stone staircase and knocked breathlessly on the heavy door of the Abbot's study.

"Enter!"

"You sent for me, Abbot?"

"Indeed. It's high time we launched another fund-raising expedition to London. Whom can we spare?"

It was the practice of the monastery to send raiding parties in mufti to exact contributions from the dilettantes in the London clubs.

"If you can't go yourself, Abbot, Brother Lucius is generally lucky."

"Not Lucius," said the Abbot. "He's still working on the tax returns. Do you think Brother Zac is past it?"

"No, indeed. And Brother Damien perhaps?"

"A blend of age and youth? Very well," declared the Abbot, picking up a cigar from a box on his desk, then changing his mind and putting it back again.

"It's a long time since I've seen a cigar, Abbot," remarked Brother Fabius. "I used to smoke them quite often, you know."

"My mind is made up. You will lead the expedition and Brothers Zac and Damien will make up the party."

"I don't often get the chance to smoke one now."

"You'll be staying at my brother's hotel in South Kensington; he offers special rates if three people share a room."

At 8 a.m. the following day the raiding party stood ready in the courtyard. Brother Zac wore old-fashioned knickerbockers. Brother Fabius sported a hacking jacket and a green pork-pie hat. Brother Damien had been to Brother Xavier for a futuristic hairstyle and was garbed in a leather jacket, faded jeans and studded boots.

"Damn and blast!" came a cry from the depths of the Abbot's garage. "What's the matter with it this time?"

"It looks like we'll have to walk to the station," sighed Brother Zac.

"That's the Dionysius Club over there," said Brother Fabius, pointing through the heavy traffic. "The cardroom is on the second floor."

"Right," said Brother Zac. "Do they have a £5 table?"

"Well, yes, but do you think that's wise? Surely a warm-up on the £1 table first?"

"Have faith," said Brother Zac, stepping into the road to a chorus of horns and screeching brakes.

Game all, dealer South

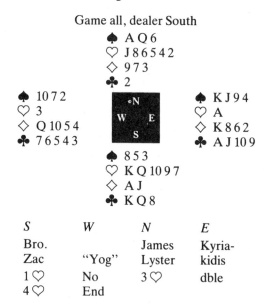

S	W	N	E
Bro.		James	Kyria-
Zac	"Yog"	Lyster	kidis
1 ♡	No	3 ♡	dble
4 ♡	End		

West, a grim-visaged Indian known as "Yog", led the seven of clubs and the Cypriot in the East seat defended accurately by withholding the ace. Since the lead was clearly top of nothing, to release the ace would set up declarer's K Q for two discards from the dummy.

Brother Zac gathered in the first trick with his king, noting that there was work to be done. East's double marked him with most of the outstanding strength, but West might hold one of the diamond honours. Heart to the ace, diamond from East, and West would come in to lead a spade through the A Q.

Instead, Brother Zac played off the ace and knave of diamonds, West winning with the queen. Declarer won the ten of spades switch with the ace, ruffed dummy's last diamond, and threw East in with a trump.

Endplayed in three suits, the Cypriot tried the ace of clubs. It was to no avail. Brother Zac ruffed in dummy, came to hand with a heart and discarded a spade on the queen of clubs.

"Well played, old chap," said North, a wavy-haired businessman in a Savile Row suit. "Can you do it if 'Yog' plays a trump instead of the ten of spades?"

"Of course," snapped the Indian. "He ruffs the diamond exit, ruffs a club, comes back to a trump and plays the club king, throwing a spade from dummy."

The Cypriot gave a dubious glance in Brother Zac's direction and turned his attention to the scoresheet. "You make it £65?" he asked.

When Brother Damien entered the Gay Cockatoo Club he was confronted by a balding man dressed in a purple shirt and camel-hair trousers.

"Well, hullo!" breathed the man, gazing admiringly at Brother Damien's blonde curls. "What gorgeous hair, my dear. Where do you have it done? Do tell me."

"Er . . . at Xavier's. Do you know it?"

"Xavier's? Can't say I do," he replied. "Are you here for the sauna or the bridge game?"

"I was hoping for a few rubbers at the £2 table, actually."

"Good, good. Julian and Aubrey are waiting for a game, so we can make up a four."

E–W game, dealer South

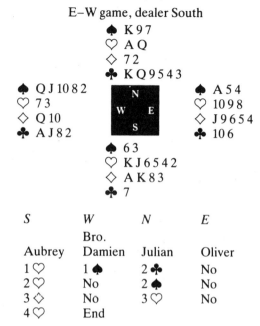

```
                    ♠ K 9 7
                    ♡ A Q
                    ◇ 7 2
                    ♣ K Q 9 5 4 3
  ♠ Q J 10 8 2                      ♠ A 5 4
  ♡ 7 3            N                ♡ 10 9 8
  ◇ Q 10        W     E             ◇ J 9 6 5 4
  ♣ A J 8 2        S                ♣ 10 6
                    ♠ 6 3
                    ♡ K J 6 5 4 2
                    ◇ A K 8 3
                    ♣ 7
```

S	W	N	E
	Bro.		
Aubrey	Damien	Julian	Oliver
1 ♡	1 ♠	2 ♣	No
2 ♡	No	2 ♠	No
3 ◇	No	3 ♡	No
4 ♡	End		

Brother Damien won the first two tricks with the queen and knave of spades and led a third round, ruffed by declarer.

"Oh, our young guest has decided to force me, has he?" said declarer, who was sporting a lime-green lambswool pullover. "There's no need. I'm always *most* willing."

"Don't be so insufferable, Aubrey," reprimanded his partner. "And that green doesn't suit you at all. I meant to tell you earlier."

"It was a present," said Aubrey, with a faraway look.

Declarer continued with a small club from hand, but Brother Damien went in with the ace and played a fourth round of spades. A little surprised at this line of defence, Aubrey ruffed in the dummy and threw a diamond from hand. East, meanwhile, disposed of his last club. These cards remained:

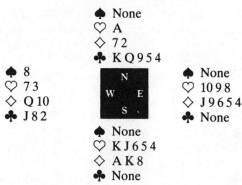

```
                    ♠ None
                    ♡ A
                    ◇ 7 2
                    ♣ K Q 9 5 4
  ♠ 8                                    ♠ None
  ♡ 7 3              N                   ♡ 1 0 9 8
  ◇ Q 10          W     E                ◇ J 9 6 5 4
  ♣ J 8 2            S                   ♣ None
                    ♠ None
                    ♡ K J 6 5 4
                    ◇ A K 8
                    ♣ None
```

The king of clubs was now ruffed by East and overruffed. Hoping that East had started with a doubleton trump, declarer crossed to the ace of trumps and tried the club queen. East ruffed again and Aubrey realised that if he overruffed he would promote a trick for West's seven of trumps and go two down. He therefore cut his losses by discarding a diamond.

"What a heavenly defence, Damien!" cried Oliver, clasping his hands in delight.

Julian, in the North seat, seemed less pleased by the outcome of the hand. "Surely you can make that, Aubrey?" he said, running his fingers through his auburn hair. "When you get the ruff-and-diskers, can't you ruff in hand and cross to one of dummy's high trumps to play the top clubs? Then if Ollie ruffs in, you can overruff and return to dummy's second trump, picking up the two outstanding trumps."

"Doesn't help, love," replied Aubrey. "The clubs aren't good. I can only get one diamond away."

As Brother Damien dealt the cards for the next hand, he wondered how his two colleagues were faring.

Brother Fabius, who had naval blood on his father's side of the family, was already several rubbers to the good at the Capstan Club.

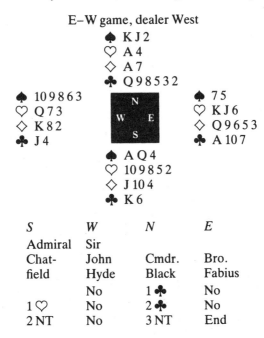

E–W game, dealer West

```
                ♠ K J 2
                ♡ A 4
                ◇ A 7
                ♣ Q 9 8 5 3 2
  ♠ 10 9 8 6 3                    ♠ 7 5
  ♡ Q 7 3        N                ♡ K J 6
  ◇ K 8 2     W     E             ◇ Q 9 6 5 3
  ♣ J 4          S                ♣ A 10 7
                ♠ A Q 4
                ♡ 10 9 8 5 2
                ◇ J 10 4
                ♣ K 6
```

S	W	N	E
Admiral	Sir		
Chat-	John	Cmdr.	Bro.
field	Hyde	Black	Fabius
	No	1 ♣	No
1 ♡	No	2 ♣	No
2 NT	No	3 NT	End

Sir John Hyde tapped the ash from his evil-smelling cigar and led the ten of spades, captured on the table.

Admiral Chatfield, who had a brilliant career behind him, including five victories in the Navy Open Pairs, now led a club to the king, which held. Hoping for a doubleton ace on his right, he ducked the next round of clubs, leaving West on lead.

A spade continuation was clearly futile, so Sir John turned his attention to the other unbid suit, switching to a small diamond. Brother Fabius, sitting East, won with the queen and paused briefly to assess the defensive prospects. Surely declarer had at least ◇ J x x for his no-trump bid, so an unthinking diamond return would at best leave the suit blocked. There was only one hope left and Brother Fabius, quick to spot it, spun the king of hearts boldly onto the table. The Admiral, hoping for a block in hearts, had to capture immediately to avoid a switch back to diamonds, but when he

[70]

cleared the club suit the defenders took their two heart tricks to put him one down.

"A damned bad lie of the cards," scowled the Admiral. "Give East a club less and I'd have made an overtrick."

"True, Admiral," conceded Brother Fabius, "but surely you should play the queen on the second round of clubs."

"Poppycock!" declared the Admiral. "Put the queen on when I know you have the ace? That would give up the only chance of picking up the clubs for one loser."

"Yes, but I can't attack the diamonds effectively from my side," Brother Fabius pointed out.

"How come we've never met you before?" enquired the Admiral sharply. "Where are you based, man?"

"Er . . . down in Hampshire, actually."

"We had a chap from Hursley Village once. Is that where you come from?"

"Never heard of it," insisted Brother Fabius. "That's not in Hampshire, surely?"

"Do you know what I think?" exclaimed the Admiral, his face infused with rage. "We've got another of those DAMNED MONKS in our midst!"

"It's not true," stammered Brother Fabius. "I'm a qualified master gunner and . . ."

"REPEL BOARDERS!" cried the Admiral, as Brother Fabius made a desperate run for the exit. "That's it, lads. Off with his trousers!"

A few days later the Abbot was waiting for them at the station in his ancient Austin Seven. He was so delighted at the extent of their plunder that he suggested stopping off at a local hostelry to celebrate.

"St. Titus himself would have been proud of you," he declared, giving each monk in turn an unusually warm smile. "Now, to business. Landlord! A pint and three halves of best bitter, if you please!"

15

Bridge Behind Bars

The Monastery of St. Titus made every effort to be self-sufficient as far as meat, grain, fruit, vegetables and dairy produce were concerned. Indeed many of the monks worked such long hours towards this end that they were forced to be non-players. All the time they could spare from earthly toil was consumed by religious devotions.

Those monks who had made the major sacrifice of giving up bridge were much admired and respected. Everyone was especially quick to praise their excellent produce in order to give them the same sense of pride and satisfaction that their colleagues achieved at the bridge table.

One important exception was Brother Fabius, who ran the monastery piggery so efficiently that he was a frequent visitor to the cardroom and had in fact made occasional appearances in the monastery first team.

"Ah, Brother Fabius! Most excellent pork chops at dinner last night," said the Abbot as they met in the cloisters one sunny morning. "Extremely succulent, I must say."

"Most kind of you to say so, Abbot. They were from one of our last Large White porkers, actually."

"Do you still smoke heavily?" continued the Abbot, changing the subject abruptly.

"Er . . . well, I'm er . . . trying to cut down on it, and . . ."

"Then·do so," declared the Abbot. "I want you fit for the match tomorrow afternoon. You may smoke then."

The following day the Abbot's heavily-loaded Austin Seven set off at high speed in a westerly direction and soon arrived at Ivyglade Prison. As the car passed through the stone portals, the Abbot reflected that his preparations for this final of the County Men's Teams knockout had been well contrived. All four members of the team had been given a dispensation to miss the early morning prayer, so that they could lie in till 6 a.m. and be well rested for the match.

The Abbot had also had the prison team watched twice. Learning that their captain, Lennie Royson, had an intense dislike of cigarette smoke, he had immediately drafted Brother Fabius, a 60-a-day man, into the team for the final.

"Good day to you, Governor," said the Abbot to the lean and harassed-looking man who greeted them on arrival. "I trust you'll see your way to releasing us again when the match is over."

"What? Ah, I see. Very amusing, Abbot," replied the Governor with a forced smile. "Unfortunately our team will not be at full strength today. Our best four decided to take advantage of the away draw in the semi-final, and only two of them have been recaptured."

Two card-tables had been set up in the prison dining hall, and amid the exotic atmosphere of disinfectant and chip-fat vapour the final was soon under way. Skilful unblocking by three of the monastery players led to a game swing on the following hand.

E–W game, dealer South

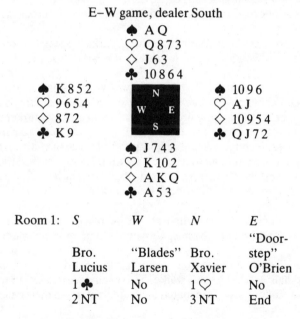

```
                    ♠ A Q
                    ♡ Q 8 7 3
                    ◇ J 6 3
                    ♣ 10 8 6 4
   ♠ K 8 5 2                        ♠ 10 9 6
   ♡ 9 6 5 4          N             ♡ A J
   ◇ 8 7 2         W     E          ◇ 10 9 5 4
   ♣ K 9              S             ♣ Q J 7 2
                    ♠ J 7 4 3
                    ♡ K 10 2
                    ◇ A K Q
                    ♣ A 5 3
```

Room 1:	S	W	N	E
				"Door-step"
	Bro.	"Blades"	Bro.	O'Brien
	Lucius	Larsen	Xavier	
	1 ♣	No	1 ♡	No
	2 NT	No	3 NT	End

West led the two of spades and dummy's queen held the trick. Brother Lucius played a heart from dummy, and when East put in the ace he made the essential unblock of the ten from hand. East returned a spade, but Brother Lucius could now pick up the hearts to score an easy game.

"An expert might have played the ace from A J 9," he remarked afterwards, "but that was unlikely on this occasion. Such a player would doubtless have avoided apprehension by the Law."

The same contract was reached in the other room, where the bidding went:

Room 2:	S	W	N	E
	Lennie	The	"Grasser"	Bro.
	Royson	Abbot	Harris	Fabius
	1 NT	No	3 NT	End

Again a spade was led and taken in the dummy, Brother Fabius unblocking the ten. As Royson led a small heart from the table, a waft of strange-smelling acrid smoke caught his nostrils, and he looked up with a murderous expression.

"What the devil are you smoking? Home-made herbal fags or something?"

"No, they are Galvanos extra-strong Turkish Specials," replied Brother Fabius, going in with the ace of hearts. "May I offer you one?"

Snorting his refusal, Royson followed with a small heart, and Brother Fabius played back the nine of spades to dummy's ace. When a heart to the king dropped East's knave, Royson regretted his failure to unblock the ten at trick 2. As the only remaining chance was to endplay West he now played his ace of clubs, but the Abbot was alert enough to unblock his king. Royson cashed the ten of hearts and the three top diamonds, but whether he exited with a club or a spade the defenders were in a position to claim the balance.

"Grasser" Harris brought out a little black pocket-book and noted down the hand. The misplay would be common knowledge by nightfall.

At half-time the monastery team led by 15 IMPs. Early in the second half Brother Fabius walked into an unnecessary 800 penalty and the Abbot judged the match to be about level when he dealt the following hand:

N–S game, dealer West

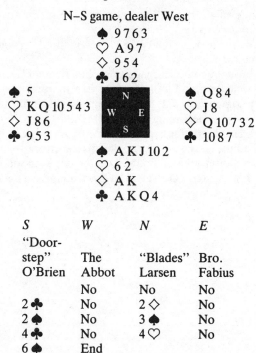

```
                    ♠ 9 7 6 3
                    ♡ A 9 7
                    ◇ 9 5 4
                    ♣ J 6 2
♠ 5                                   ♠ Q 8 4
♡ K Q 10 5 4 3         N              ♡ J 8
◇ J 8 6            W       E          ◇ Q 10 7 3 2
♣ 9 5 3                S              ♣ 10 8 7
                    ♠ A K J 10 2
                    ♡ 6 2
                    ◇ A K
                    ♣ A K Q 4
```

S	W	N	E
"Door-step" O'Brien	The Abbot	"Blades" Larsen	Bro. Fabius
	No	No	No
2♣	No	2◇	No
2♠	No	3♠	No
4♣	No	4♡	No
6♠	End		

The king of hearts lead was captured in dummy by the declarer, a ruddy-faced jovial individual who until recently had been managing director of the Royal Dublin Insurance Company. Hoping to gain some information on the lie of the trump suit, he now made the strange-looking play of a diamond to the ace, followed by a trump from table.

"Er ... you're in hand, aren't you?" remarked Brother Fabius, sitting East.

"Is that so?" replied O'Brien innocently. "It makes not a drop of difference. Oi'm playin' the spade ace anyway."

Taking note of East's reluctance to allow a trump lead from dummy, O'Brien played a club to the table and followed with a finesse in trumps. When this succeeded he claimed twelve tricks.

"Good view, partner," muttered North with a thin-lipped smile.

"Oi rarely go wrong with that combination," replied O'Brien, filling in his scorecard with a flourish.

The last few hands were uneventful and the Abbot strode grimly back to compare scores.

"What happened on board 28?" he enquired anxiously as he entered the room.

"Oh, I brought home six spades," replied Brother Lucius. "West opened a weak two, so I took the right view in trumps."

A hasty comparison and two recounts revealed that the monastery team had scraped home by just 2 IMPs.

"Phew! Thank goodness my 800 didn't cost us the match," said Brother Fabius, taking a long draw on his last cigarette.

"The result was never in doubt," declared the Abbot, raising his eyes towards heaven. "Good will always triumph over evil."

PART II

Interlude in Africa

16

Under the Cola Tree

It was an intensely hot afternoon and the jungle clearing was seething with activity. On the far side some men were engaged in chopping wood, while near the huts the women of the tribe were congregated, grinding maize and preparing the evening meal.

Seemingly unaware of all this, two missionaries and two of the tribe were about to enjoy an open-air bridge game under the large cola tree next to Brother Luke's hut.

"Usual stakes, five beads a hundred?" enquired Brother Tobias, who was already dealing the first hand.

Love all, dealer South

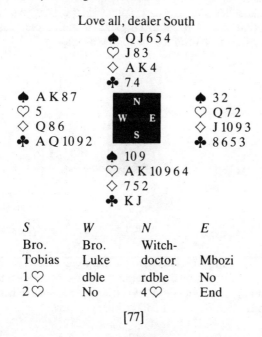

```
                    ♠ Q J 6 5 4
                    ♡ J 8 3
                    ♢ A K 4
                    ♣ 7 4
  ♠ A K 8 7                        ♠ 3 2
  ♡ 5              N               ♡ Q 7 2
  ♢ Q 8 6       W     E            ♢ J 10 9 3
  ♣ A Q 10 9 2     S               ♣ 8 6 5 3
                    ♠ 10 9
                    ♡ A K 10 9 6 4
                    ♢ 7 5 2
                    ♣ K J
```

S	W	N	E
Bro.	Bro.	Witch-	
Tobias	Luke	doctor	Mbozi
1 ♡	dble	rdble	No
2 ♡	No	4 ♡	End

Brother Tobias, who had been instructed by the Abbot to convert the Bozwambi tribe to the Acol system, opened the auction with one heart.

Brother Luke doubled in the West seat, and when the witch-doctor redoubled, Brother Tobias removed himself to two hearts. Unknown to him, this was quite a strong bid in the Banana Club system previously favoured by this tribe, and the witch-doctor raised him straight to game.

Brother Luke cashed a top spade, and the witch-doctor tabled his cards.

"If de hands fit good, we mebbe am havin' a slam here," he commented. "I always a bit cautious on de first hand."

"Oh, er . . . yes. Most commendable restraint," replied Brother Tobias.

Catching sight of dummy's threatening spade suit, Brother Luke switched hastily to a small diamond, which was won on the table. Helped by the bidding, Brother Tobias let the knave of trumps ride. He then drew two more rounds of trumps before leading his ten of spades. When Brother Luke defended well by ducking the spade, declarer overtook in dummy and ruffed a spade back, hoping the suit would divide 3–3.

This plan failed, but Brother Tobias, kicking away a couple of chickens that had run squawking under the table, cashed his remaining trumps to produce the following ending:

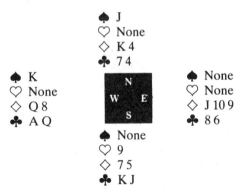

On the last trump West discarded a diamond. Declarer crossed to the king of diamonds and led dummy's knave of spades, throwing his last diamond from hand. West won and had reluctantly to concede a trick to Brother Tobias's king of clubs.

"Dat most excellent play, bwana," exclaimed the witch-doctor, his feathered head-dress rustling with appreciation. "We are calling dis play de triple python, because de opponent am most nastily crushed in three places."

"Bwana Luke!" cried Mbozi angrily. "Five clubs am only one or mebbe two down, and in Banana Club system we most easily am reachin' dis contract. Dis makin' me extra cross because Bozwambi tribe am always have been extremely keen on sacrifices. Of any sort."

"That's quite enough of that, Mbozi," said Brother Tobias, wiping his perspiring forehead authoritatively. "One of the hallmarks of modern civilisation is an unwavering politeness to one's bridge partner."

"Why don't dat applyin' to you too, bwana?" asked Mbozi. "Yesterday when Bwana Luke was doublin' dat four hearts you most fearsome angry. You call him a blidderin' clodpole, whatever dat is."

"Believe me, I have already done penance for that," replied Brother Tobias. "I had provocation, I say no more. Now let's continue the game."

E–W game, dealer North

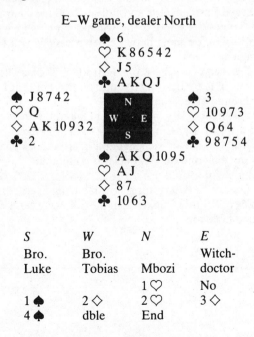

```
              ♠ 6
              ♡ K 8 6 5 4 2
              ◇ J 5
              ♣ A K Q J
♠ J 8 7 4 2                    ♠ 3
♡ Q                            ♡ 10 9 7 3
◇ A K 10 9 3 2                 ◇ Q 6 4
♣ 2                            ♣ 9 8 7 5 4
              ♠ A K Q 10 9 5
              ♡ A J
              ◇ 8 7
              ♣ 10 6 3
```

S	W	N	E
Bro.	Bro.		Witch-
Luke	Tobias	Mbozi	doctor
		1 ♡	No
1 ♠	2 ◇	2 ♡	3 ◇
4 ♣	dble	End	

Brother Tobias's double was far from cast-iron, but he had no wish to leave the decision to the notoriously volatile judgement of the witch-doctor. When Brother Tobias cashed two diamonds and exited with a heart, Brother Luke brushed away a vicious-looking mosquito from the sleeve of his cassock and paused for thought.

West surely had five trumps for his double, and since the heart queen looked every inch a singleton, he was marked with 5–1–5–2 or 5–1–6–1 distribution. If declarer simply played four rounds of trumps immediately, West would lock him in dummy and subsequently claim a second trump trick. It was necessary therefore to extract West's clubs before playing on trumps, but how many clubs did West have?

"Small heart please, Mbozi," requested Brother Luke, suddenly emerging from his trance.

"Dis not duplicate. You are a lazy-bwana," reprimanded Mbozi, who nevertheless leaned forward and played the card.

Brother Luke won the heart lead in hand, cashed just one club and then played four rounds of trumps, discarding the three remaining club honours from dummy. When in with the knave of spades, West could exit only with a trump or a diamond. The last trump squeezed East in hearts and clubs to land the contract.

"Bwana Tobias!" exploded the witch-doctor, who was sitting East. "Dis is bein' de most pathetic defence since you lettin' dat 3 NT through last week."

"Well, I'm very sorry," replied Brother Tobias meekly. "I thought I'd be able to lock him in dummy. Is it better if I continue with a third round of diamonds, then?"

"Dat equal most useless, bwana," said the witch-doctor, stretching out an arm for a passing tarantula, which he consumed with relish. "But if you playin' de singleton heart at trick 2, den later crossin' to my diamond queen, declarer go tumblin' down. I must havin' de queen for my bid, isn't it?"

A while later, with two vultures now kibitzing from a low branch of the cola tree, Brother Tobias dealt the following cards round the sun-bleached table top.

Love all, dealer South

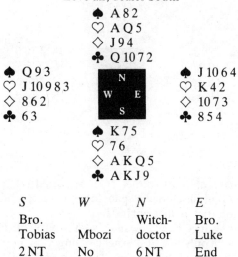

```
              ♠ A 8 2
              ♡ A Q 5
              ◇ J 9 4
              ♣ Q 10 7 2
♠ Q 9 3                      ♠ J 10 6 4
♡ J 10 9 8 3                 ♡ K 4 2
◇ 8 6 2                      ◇ 10 7 3
♣ 6 3                        ♣ 8 5 4
              ♠ K 7 5
              ♡ 7 6
              ◇ A K Q 5
              ♣ A K J 9
```

S	W	N	E
Bro.		Witch-	Bro.
Tobias	Mbozi	doctor	Luke
2 NT	No	6 NT	End

Mbozi led the knave of hearts and the witch-doctor tabled his 13-count.

"I goin' fetch some icy drinks, bwana," he said, rising to his feet. "De sun-god most fierce today."

Brother Tobias gave the witch-doctor a frown of disapproval but was too concerned with the play to enter into a theological discussion. Six clubs would have been easy, but what were his chances in no-trumps? His first thought was to duck the opening lead, but he saw that if East held a doubleton king of hearts, or king of hearts and all the spades, he would lose nothing by taking the first trick. So he went up with the ace of hearts and ran both the minor suits. At trick 9 these cards were still exposed to the jungle sun (*see over*):

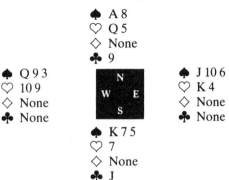

♠ A 8
♡ Q 5
◇ None
♣ 9

♠ Q 9 3   ♠ J 10 6
♡ 10 9   ♡ K 4
◇ None   ◇ None
♣ None   ♣ None

♠ K 7 5
♡ 7
◇ None
♣ J

On the knave of clubs neither defender could safely release a heart so they both discarded a spade, thereby presenting declarer with his twelfth trick in that suit instead.

"Dat most strange hand, bwana," said Mbozi. "It like double squeeze but with only two suits instead of three."

"By St. Christopher, you're right," exclaimed Brother Tobias. It never ceased to amaze him that while the bidding of the Bozwambi tribe waᶜ ᵉxtremely wild and primitive, their understanding of cardplay was unexpectedly good.

"Ah, the drinks have arrived," said Brother Luke breezily. "What have you brought for us?"

"Half-pint each of de best palm gin and coconut milk," replied the witch-doctor, setting four earthenware mugs on the table. "Couldn't gettin' any ice, though. Magic cold-box you bringin' from England not workin' too well since I took de door off."

They were all busily sipping their drinks when a large spear descended from the sky, shattering the card table into a mass of splinters.

"Dat am war-spear of Zbolwumba tribe!" cried Mbozi, leaping to his feet in alarm.

"The Lord will protect us," said Brother Tobias confidently. "Let's agree the score. 960 to us, is it? Don't forget 300 for game in an unfinished rubber."

17

Brother Luke's Parrot

"You know the parrot that young Mjubu gave me a couple of months ago?" said Brother Luke, sitting out in the sun after a heavy lunch.

"Yes, what's happened? Has it died?" asked Brother Tobias, not sounding very interested.

> "Passer mortuus est meae puellae,
> Passer, deliciae meae puellae,"

murmured Brother Luke, recalling Catullus.

Brother Tobias, who was no great scholar, yawned non-committally and began to doze off.

"Of course it hasn't died," continued Brother Luke. "I'm trying to teach it to play bridge. I hold up a hand outside his cage, and if he makes the right bid I reward him with some birdseed. Come into my hut for a moment and I'll show you how he's getting on."

As they entered the relative coolness of his grass hut, Brother Luke picked up the pack of cards lying on his table and dealt the following hand:

> ♠ A Q 6
> ♡ K 10 9 4
> ♢ K 9 6 3
> ♣ 10 4

He held it up to the bamboo cage, but the parrot showed little interest, continuing to preen his blue and yellow feathers disdainfully.

"Yes, he's rather a cautious bidder," explained Brother Luke. "He obviously doesn't think it's worth an opening bid."

"Well, give him a better hand," said Brother Tobias, eager to see the parrot perform.

Brother Luke dealt another hand and pressed it against the bars of the parrot's cage.

> ♠ K Q
> ♡ A K Q 10 9 7
> ♢ A J 10
> ♣ A 6

"One crub!" squawked the parrot, obviously expecting some birdseed for his splendid efforts.

"What does he play? Precision?" asked Brother Tobias, peering disapprovingly into the cage.

"Brother Tobias doesn't play Precision," Brother Luke informed the parrot. "Try again, will you?"

"One heart!" screeched the parrot.

Brother Luke let a few seeds fall into the cage, then walked out into the scorching sun again. "It was an obvious two-club bid," he muttered to Brother Tobias. "Sometimes he just tries to annoy me."

One humid afternoon a few weeks later, most of the tribe were out on an elephant hunt and the two missionaries remaining in the village were desperate for a game of bridge. With some difficulty they managed to recruit Mrs. Mbozi, who had never actually played before but claimed to have watched the game a couple of times. The four was completed by Brother Luke's parrot, who had been improving steadily under his owner's painstaking tuition.

"The sides seem fairly evenly balanced," whispered Brother Luke, out of Mrs. Mbozi's earshot. "Shall we make it the usual stakes?"

Brother Tobias nodded his agreement and proceeded to deal the first hand.

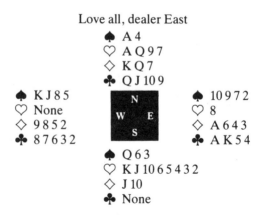

Love all, dealer East

	♠ A 4	
	♡ A Q 9 7	
	◇ K Q 7	
	♣ Q J 10 9	
♠ K J 8 5		♠ 10 9 7 2
♡ None		♡ 8
◇ 9 8 5 2		◇ A 6 4 3
♣ 8 7 6 3 2		♣ A K 5 4
	♠ Q 6 3	
	♡ K J 10 6 5 4 3 2	
	◇ J 10	
	♣ None	

Brother Luke's Parrot

S	W	N	E
The	Mrs.	Bro.	Bro.
Parrot	Mbozi	Luke	Tobias
			No
4 ♡	No	4 NT	No
5 ♡	No	5 NT	No
6 ♡	No	7 ♡	dble

The parrot, using his beak to sort his cards into an elegant eucalyptus-wood holder carved for him by the young Mjubu, opened the bidding with four hearts. His partner responded four no-trumps and, although the parrot had not followed Brother Luke's lecture on Blackwood too closely, he nevertheless felt in his feathers that this was some sort of slam try. Casting a beady eye along the line of mediocre cards in his cardholder, the parrot signed off in five hearts. When Brother Luke persisted with five no-trumps, the parrot signed off again in *six* hearts. He looked distinctly annoyed when his partner pushed on to the grand slam regardless.

When East doubled, Brother Luke was tempted to shift the contract into no-trumps so that he could play the hand, but the prospect of being the owner and trainer of the first parrot in the world ever to make a grand slam was irresistible.

Mrs. Mbozi, who was on lead, remembered once overhearing that you should always lead a trump against a grand slam. When a diligent search of her hand failed to reveal any trumps, she chose instead the three of clubs, the fourth best of her longest suit.

The parrot, who was in the habit of making his plays from dummy by strutting across the table and picking up the required card in his beak, ruffed East's ace of clubs and crossed back to the table with the ace of trumps. He then led the queen of clubs and threw a diamond on it when East did not cover. Another club followed, covered and ruffed, and the parrot re-entered dummy with the seven of trumps to discard his last diamond on the established club.

The king of diamonds followed, and Brother Tobias in the East seat, who could guess from the fall of declarer's cards that he was now out of diamonds, defended well by not covering the king. The parrot discarded a losing spade and, as if guided by some supernatural jungle force, continued unerringly with the queen of diamonds.

This was covered and ruffed, but Mrs. Mbozi, sitting West, was now saddled with the responsibility of guarding both diamonds and spades, and when the parrot ran the trump suit she proved unequal to the task.

"You are a marvellous, wonderful bird!" cried Brother Luke, tears of gratitude and affection coming to his eyes. "Please excuse me for a moment," he said, rising to his feet. "I'm just going to my hut to fetch the box of birdseed."

"I'd have thought it was worth more than a beakful of that tasteless birdseed, to make a slam like that," muttered the parrot. "You may deal the next hand for me," he added, nudging the cards towards Mrs. Mbozi.

Mjubu's First Hand

The young males of the Bozwambi tribe were forbidden to play bridge before undergoing their initiation rites at the age of fifteen. They were then taken to a secret location, far out in the jungle, and subjected to a week's intensive instruction from the tribal witch-doctor. The rites reached their climax when the initiates, daubed with red and black dye, returned to the village to take part in their first ceremonial rubbers.

Since the arrival of the team of English missionaries led by Brother Tobias, the Bozwambi tribe, former cannibals, had ceased to use their traditional packs of cards which had hearts, livers, kidneys and brains as the suit symbols. So it was with a brand new pack of Waddington Number Ones that Brother Luke dealt this hand, the very first that the young Mjubu had ever played.

Love all, dealer South

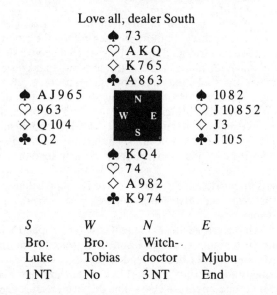

	♠ 7 3	
	♡ A K Q	
	◇ K 7 6 5	
	♣ A 8 6 3	
♠ A J 9 6 5		♠ 10 8 2
♡ 9 6 3		♡ J 10 8 5 2
◇ Q 10 4		◇ J 3
♣ Q 2		♣ J 10 5
	♠ K Q 4	
	♡ 7 4	
	◇ A 9 8 2	
	♣ K 9 7 4	

S	W	N	E
Bro.	Bro.	Witch-.	
Luke	Tobias	doctor	Mjubu
1 NT	No	3 NT	End

Brother Tobias led the six of spades, dummy following with the three. For reasons best known to himself Mjubu contributed the two, and declarer's king won the trick.

Noting that there were a healthy eight tricks already on view, Brother Luke crossed to a heart and led a small club, intending to duck the trick to West, the safe hand. Mjubu followed with the knave and when declarer, perforce, won the king, Brother Tobias was quick to dispense with his queen.

Taking a sip of the fermented guava juice always provided on these occasions, Brother Luke decided to postpone any further manoeuvring in the club suit. Instead he crossed to another heart and led a low diamond towards his hand. Once again Mjubu went in with the knave without apparent thought. Declarer had to win the trick and West tossed in the queen.

Brother Luke blinked in disbelief and reached absently for his glass which proved, annoyingly, to be empty.

"You like 'nother drink, bwana?" offered Mjubu eagerly. In common with the other initiates, he had not been allowed to taste this powerful concoction before and was therefore glad of an opportunity to refill his own glass.

"No, thank you, Mjubu. Well, yes, I will in a minute, but let me finish this hand first."

What on earth was going on in the minors? If East had started with knave-ten to three or more in each minor the situation was hopeless, thought Brother Luke. His best chance was surely that East held knave-ten alone in one of the suits and that West, with no count on the suit, had unblocked from queen to three.

Hoping for the best, Brother Luke cashed the king of diamonds and the ace of clubs, bringing forth just a trickle of small cards. Brother Luke now had to guess which of the outstanding minor suit tens West held, if any. A notoriously unlucky guesser, he opted for the club suit, and Mjubu fired through a spade to send the game two down.

"A sensational defence, Mjubu!" cried Brother Tobias. "And to think that was the first hand you've ever played. It's quite unbelievable."

"De witch-doctor, he most excellent teacher," replied Mjubu, his nose-ring glistening with enthusiasm. "All week he am drummin' into us de four secret rules: to lead always de fourth best, to play always high in de second seat and low in de third seat and, most important dis one, to return every time de partner's suit. Dese rules certainly am seem to workin' most acceptable."

"No, no, Mjubu. You've got it hopelessly wrong," said Brother

Luke in an exasperated voice. "You must play low in the second seat and high in the third. Isn't that so, Brother Tobias?"

"There are exceptions to every rule," Brother Tobias replied sententiously. "For example, you should perhaps have played the seven of spades from dummy on the first trick. If Mjubu still sees fit to follow with the two, you make the contract easily."

19

The Abbot and the Grasshopper

"Bozwambi Airlines am announcin' de arrival of flight BOZ1 from London," blared the loudspeaker through a haze of static. Brother Tobias rose to his feet and soon spotted the perspiring figure of the Abbot elbowing his way through the crowd.

"Welcome to Africa, Abbot!" declared Brother Tobias with a warm smile. "Come this way, the jeep is outside and ..."

"Flight BOZ2 will be leavin' for London next Wednesday," interrupted the loudspeaker.

"... it's only a two-hour drive to the Mission," continued Brother Tobias. "We've made splendid progress since your last visit and the natives are so looking forward to playing against you."

"Yes. Well, it's all part of our duty," replied the Abbot, beginning to regret that he had travelled in a heavy woollen habit.

Later that evening a table was set up in Brother Tobias's grass hut, and the game was soon under way.

E–W game, dealer South

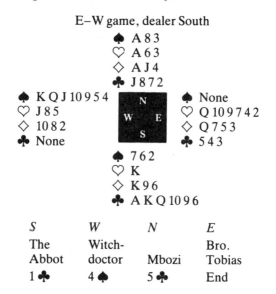

```
                  ♠ A 8 3
                  ♡ A 6 3
                  ♢ A J 4
                  ♣ J 8 7 2
♠ K Q J 10 9 5 4      N        ♠ None
♡ J 8 5          W       E     ♡ Q 10 9 7 4 2
♢ 10 8 2                       ♢ Q 7 5 3
♣ None               S        ♣ 5 4 3
                  ♠ 7 6 2
                  ♡ K
                  ♢ K 9 6
                  ♣ A K Q 10 9 6
```

S	W	N	E
The	Witch-		Bro.
Abbot	doctor	Mbozi	Tobias
1 ♣	4 ♠	5 ♣	End

The Abbot opened the auction with one club and the witch-

"Well, there's nothing I can do about it," declared Brother Xavier. "If I try to knock out his entry by returning the king of diamonds, declarer just unblocks the knave from hand."

"What's wrong with the nine of spades at trick 2?" asked Brother Lucius with a patient sigh.

"Oh, I see. Did you have the ten, then?"

"Yes, and if declarer ducks the spade I can overtake and continue our attack on the diamond ace from the correct side."

Soon afterwards Brother Xavier dealt the cards as follows:

Game all, dealer South

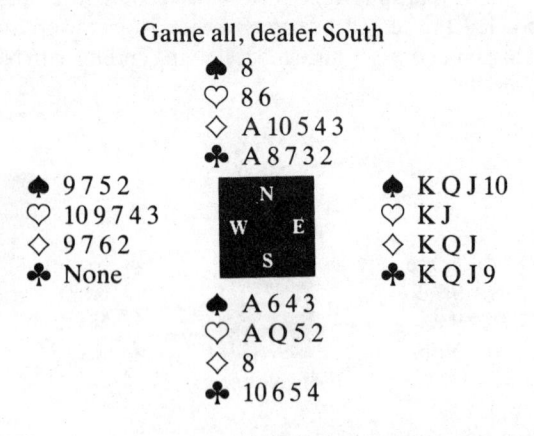

♠ 8
♡ 8 6
◇ A 10 5 4 3
♣ A 8 7 3 2

♠ 9 7 5 2
♡ 10 9 7 4 3
◇ 9 7 6 2
♣ None

♠ K Q J 10
♡ K J
◇ K Q J
♣ K Q J 9

♠ A 6 4 3
♡ A Q 5 2
◇ 8
♣ 10 6 5 4

Viewing his dismal collection in the West seat, the Abbot opened the bidding with a confident one club. This diversion was, after all, fairly safe with Brother Anthony as partner.

Brother Anthony, sitting East gazed wistfully at his 22-count and prepared himself to deliver the almost imperceptible shake of the head that had formed his bidding methods for the past thirty-odd years.

"Surely my partner dealt this one," said Brother Lucius, alert as ever. "Your bid was out of turn, Abbot, but there's no penalty if Brother Xavier passes."

"One club," said Brother Xavier, who knew the ruling. "Since I've made a bid, Abbot, your partner must pass throughout. Harsh as it is, I'm afraid we must enforce the letter of the Law."

"Come, come, partner," said Brother Lucius, much amused. "Since this is a game between friends, let's waive the penalty."

The Abbot passed and Brother Lucius, in the North seat, raised his partner to five clubs.

Brother Anthony re-scanned his 22-count, seething with anger. They were making a mockery of him. They were insulting the venerable Eustacian order and implying that nearly four hundred years of silence had all been in vain. The time had come to teach them a sharp lesson.

"Double!" he said, noting with interest that, since taking his vows at a tender age, his voice had broken.

Only the ticking of the Abbot's grandfather clock interrupted the stunned silence that followed. After a few moments all passed and the Abbot led the ten of hearts. Brother Xavier won and cross-ruffed at high speed to produce the following ending with North, the dummy, on play:

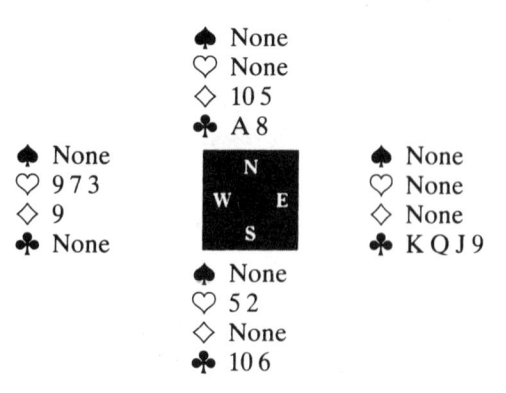

```
              ♠ None
              ♡ None
              ♢ 10 5
              ♣ A 8
♠ None                        ♠ None
♡ 9 7 3      N                ♡ None
♢ 9       W     E             ♢ None
♣ None        S               ♣ K Q J 9
              ♠ None
              ♡ 5 2
              ♢ None
              ♣ 10 6
```

Brother Anthony was forced to ruff the diamond high and exit with another high trump to the ace. Dummy's last diamond now promoted declarer's ten of trumps and amazingly the game was home.

"What in the name of St. Titus do you mean by breaking your vow of silence, just to double a cold game?" demanded the Abbot with a most fearsome glare.

Offering no answer, Brother Anthony rose to his feet. Then, pulling up the cowl of his cloak, he walked sadly to the door and out into the unforgiving night.

doctor, notorious for his overbidding, made a vulnerable four-spade overcall. Mbozi, sitting North, could sense an easy 800 or so, but like every other native in the tribe he never dared double the witch-doctor. Not with a wife and five children at home; it wasn't worth the risk. Instead, much to the relief of Brother Tobias in the East seat, he settled for a mundane five clubs and this call closed the auction. The witch-doctor led the king of spades and down went the dummy.

"Thank you very much, Moses," said the Abbot, who had been tactfully requested to show indulgence to the natives, whatever the provocation. "Most accurately bid, if I may say so."

"My name not Moses, bwana. It is Mbozi, like in de town-name Mbozdinga."

But the Abbot was not listening; he was busy planning the play of the hand. Since East was obviously void in spades, the Abbot ducked the first trick and put up the ace at trick 2. This was the only safe way to rectify the count and leave all his menaces intact. If West had started with no more than two hearts a straightforward double squeeze would now result. East ruffed the ace of spades and returned a heart, and the Abbot ran the trump suit to produce the following ending:

```
                    ♠ 8
                    ♡ 6
                    ♢ A J 4
                    ♣ None
     ♠ J          ┌─────────┐      ♠ None
     ♡ J          │    N    │      ♡ Q 9
     ♢ 10 8 2     │ W     E │      ♢ Q 7 5
     ♣ None       │    S    │      ♣ None
                  └─────────┘
                    ♠ None
                    ♡ None
                    ♢ K 9 6
                    ♣ 10 9
```

On the ten of clubs the witch-doctor, who had a count on declarer's hand, shifted uneasily in his uncushioned bamboo seat. If he discarded his heart, declarer's last trump would clearly complete a double squeeze, so he had to throw a diamond. The knave of diamonds was discarded from the table and East threw a heart. On the last trump West had once more to play a diamond, and the

[91]

Abbot triumphantly made the last three diamond tricks by crossing to the ace and finessing the nine on the way back.

"Abbot-bwana! How you so sure my partner have no spades?" asked the witch-doctor, rolling his eyes suspiciously.

"Not very difficult, considering the bidding," laughed the Abbot.

"I often am makin' dat bid wid only six trumps," persisted the witch-doctor.

The Abbot could summon up little interest in discussing the bidding of the hand. Why hadn't everyone praised his superb dummy play? They always did back at the monastery in England.

"Don't needin' to duck de spade ace anyhow," muttered Mbozi. "Just ruffin' out de hearts and playin' three rounds of diamonds brings home de bacon."

"As the cards lie, that is true," replied the Abbot. "But mine was a sharper line of play."

Outside the hut the jungle noises were reaching their climax and a full moon lit the sky. Inside, meanwhile, the oil lamps were flickering and the players were halfway through their fourth rubber.

N–S game, dealer West

```
                    ♠ 7 6 2
                    ♡ K 10 7 2
                    ◇ A 10 7 4
                    ♣ K 8
   ♠ 10                             ♠ K Q J 9 3
   ♡ 9 5 3          N              ♡ Q J 4
   ◇ J 9 3 2      W   E            ◇ 8 5
   ♣ 9 6 5 3 2       S              ♣ Q 7 4
                    ♠ A 8 5 4
                    ♡ A 8 6
                    ◇ K Q 6
                    ♣ A J 10
```

S	W	N	E
Witch-		Bro.	The
doctor	Mbozi	Tobias	Abbot
	No	No	1 ♠
3 NT	No	4 NT	End

The Abbot made a light opening bid in the third seat and the witch-doctor made a wild leap to three no-trumps, a disgraceful

overbid. Brother Tobias raised him to four, and the witch-doctor, who still felt he had something to spare, spent some time assessing the slam prospects. When he reluctantly decided against bidding on, Mbozi led the ten of spades.

"My fault if dere is a slam here," apologised the witch-doctor. "I always a bit cautious at dis vulnerability."

East overtook his partner's lead, and the witch-doctor won the first trick with the ace. The king of clubs was followed by a successful club finesse and the ace of clubs. Now the witch-doctor needed only to bring in the diamond suit to make the contract.

When he cashed the king-queen and led the six, West followed with the nine and a large grasshopper jumped on the table.

"Leave it to me," said the Abbot menacingly, moving a huge hand slowly towards the creature.

"No, no, Abbot-bwana! Don't kill him," cried the witch-doctor. "De Bozwambi tribe never kill de grasshopper-god, it much nasty bad luck."

"Grasshopper-god? What nonsense," replied the Abbot. "I'm surprised you don't clamp down on this sort of superstition, Brother Tobias."

The witch-doctor, meanwhile, had moved the ace and ten of diamonds towards the centre of the table.

"Watch, Abbot-bwana," he said dramatically. "De grasshopper-god will jump on de card I should play to dis trick. Dis show you how clever he is."

All eyes were focused on the grasshopper, who remained stationary for a couple of seconds and then made an almighty leap onto dummy's king of hearts.

"A revoke!" declared the Abbot in such a loud voice that the grasshopper took off again, this time landing squarely in the middle of the diamond ace. The Abbot discarded the three of spades on this card and the witch-doctor, claiming that the grasshopper had been affected by outside influences, brushed the creature to the ground.

When the witch-doctor exited with the ten of diamonds to West's knave and West cashed his two master clubs, the Abbot was forced to unguard one of the majors and the contract was made.

"Why the deuce did you cash both those clubs, Moses?" cried the Abbot. "Wasn't it obvious you would squeeze me?"

"Don't go blamin' me," sulked Mbozi. "I takin' three tricks wid only one point in my hand and you, wid openin' bid, not even managin' one."

"It wouldn't make any difference anyhow, Abbot," said Brother Tobias. "If Mbozi does exit with a heart instead of cashing the last club, this is the end position:

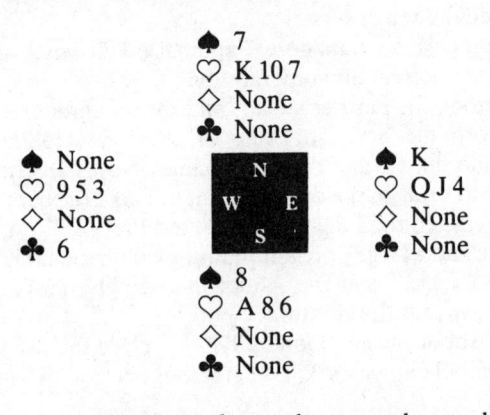

```
                    ♠ 7
                    ♡ K 10 7
                    ◇ None
                    ♣ None
  ♠ None              N          ♠ K
  ♡ 9 5 3        W        E      ♡ Q J 4
  ◇ None             S          ◇ None
  ♣ 6                            ♣ None
                    ♠ 8
                    ♡ A 8 6
                    ◇ None
                    ♣ None
```

"North covers West's card, you have to play an honour and declarer wins. Now he can simply exit with a spade and you have to lead back into dummy's heart tenace."

"You see, Abbot-bwana?" said the witch-doctor with a horrible toothless grin. "De grasshopper-god worked all dis out. Dat's why he make de safety-play of jumpin' on de ace!"

Mbozi's Postmortem

"Dere was plenty tracks of wild pig over by de swamp dis mornin'," said Mjubu excitedly. "You fancy nice piece of huntin' dis afternoon?"

"Sure sounds temptin'," replied Mbozi wistfully. "But I promised to makin' up bridge game with de white bwanas."

"Why you play dat borin' game?" asked Mjubu. "Nobody ever get killed in it."

"Dat's true," acknowledged Mbozi with a nod. "But I usually gettin' three, four glasses of white man's whisky-drink. Dat make it seem quite good game after a while."

"Are you any good at de game?" asked Mjubu, sharpening up some arrowheads with a round stone.

"I's de best player. Dem white crocodiles won't admit it, of course."

E–W game, dealer West

```
              ♠ 7 5 4
              ♡ J 8 6
              ♢ A Q 9
              ♣ K 9 6 3
♠ J 9 3                        ♠ None
♡ 9 5          N               ♡ A K Q 10 3 2
♢ 10 6 5 3 2   W   E           ♢ K 8 7 4
♣ Q 7 5        S               ♣ 10 8 2
              ♠ A K Q 10 8 6 2
              ♡ 7 4
              ♢ J
              ♣ A J 4
```

S	W	N	E
Bro.		Bro.	Witch-
Tobias	Mbozi	Luke	doctor
	No	No	1 ♡
2 ♠	No	3 ♠	4 ♡
4 ♠	No	No	dble

When the witch-doctor opened one heart, Brother Tobias's first inclination was to overcall four spades on the South cards. But recently he had spent many hours in a fruitless attempt to curb the witch-doctor's wild overbidding, and he thought that an ultra-conservative call of two spades would set him an excellent example. A few seconds later, following another overbid by the witch-doctor, Brother Tobias found himself in four spades anyway.

"Wake up, Mbozi," he said sharply. "It's your lead."

"I most wide awake and alert, bwana. I just thinkin' what lead to make," replied an affronted Mbozi. "Now, what's de contract?"

"Four spades," hissed the witch-doctor, looking as sinister as ever in his head-dress of blood-stained chicken feathers. "But I bid hearts. In fact I's biddin' hearts twice."

Mbozi led the nine of hearts and the witch-doctor played three rounds, declarer ruffing high and West throwing a diamond. One round of trumps revealed a loser in that suit, so a minor-suit finesse would be required for the contract. Still, surely even the witch-doctor was marked with both the missing minor-suit honours, having bid a vulnerable four hearts on his own. Brother Tobias put West in with the third round of trumps, won the diamond exit with dummy's ace, ruffed the nine of diamonds to return to hand and then ran the trump suit. This line would succeed if East had the queen of clubs, as expected, or if West held the queen of clubs doubleton (this would show up in the end-game since East would be forced to discard two clubs). When neither of these distributions materialised, the game was one down.

"Your overbidding is a disgrace to the tribe!" cried Brother Tobias, spinning angrily towards the witch-doctor. "What on earth did you have for all those bids?"

"I havin' most excellent four-loser hand, bwana," exclaimed the witch-doctor. "It was mos' probably a two-bid in de first place."

"Surely de contract should be makin' anyway," Mbozi muttered thoughtfully.

"You had five losers at least," persisted Brother Tobias, "and in four hearts doubled you would very likely lose control and go for a well deserved 1100."

"Yes, if declarer play off de ace of diamonds before puttin' me in," continued Mbozi, "I got no good exit card."

"Be quiet, Mbozi," said Brother Tobias. "What on earth do you know about cardplay? You've only been playing bridge for three months."

Brother Luke wisely held his peace and began to deal the next hand. He had no desire to turn Brother Tobias's sharp temper in his own direction.

Some time later the two missionaries were a game up when the following monstrous hand arrived.

N–S game, dealer South

```
                    ♠ A 8 6
                    ♡ A J 9 3 2
                    ◇ J 9 6 5 2
                    ♣ None
  ♠ K Q 9 4 2                      ♠ 10 7 5 3
  ♡ K Q 7 6         N              ♡ 10 8 5
  ◇ K Q 7 3       W   E            ◇ 8 4
  ♣ None            S              ♣ 9 7 4 3
                    ♠ J
                    ♡ 4
                    ◇ A 10
                    ♣ A K Q J 10 8 6 5 2
```

S	W	N	E
Bro.		Bro.	Witch-
Tobias	Mbozi	Luke	doctor
1 ♣	dble	rdble	1 ♠
4 NT	5 ♠	5 NT	No
7 ♣	No	No	7 ♠
7 NT	End		

Hoping once more to teach by example, Brother Tobias opened the bidding with a modest one club on the South cards. The bid was most unlikely to be passed out, he thought, particularly with the witch-doctor at the table. After a double, a redouble, and a bid of one spade from East, Brother Tobias exercised no further restraint, leaping straight into Blackwood.

Mbozi, sitting West, put in an excellent nuisance bid of five spades and Brother Luke paused to consider. What was the scheme the Abbot had taught them a few years ago back in the monastery in England? Ah yes ... pass with no aces, double with one and bid with two.

"Five no-trumps," he said, hoping that Brother Tobias would be on the same wavelength.

"Brings back memories of the Abbot standing pompously at the blackboard, doesn't it?" said Brother Tobias, unsure if his partner had remembered the approved scheme.

"Yes, indeed," smiled his partner.

Good, thought Brother Tobias, he has remembered. Unable to ask for kings now, Brother Tobias decided to pot seven clubs anyway. Even a major-suit queen in dummy should be enough.

The witch-doctor sacrificed in seven spades and Brother Tobias, unwilling to assign his spectacular club suit to defence, pressed on to seven no-trumps. Mbozi, with three king-queen leads to choose from (a rare luxury against a grand slam), eventually selected the king of diamonds.

Brother Tobias swallowed hard as he surveyed the disappointing dummy. If West had all four red honour cards, not unlikely on the bidding, it looked as if a simple red suit squeeze might give the contract. Unfortunately, though, the diamond lead prevented declarer playing off the ace of spades before running the clubs, so a simple squeeze could be ruled out. Nevertheless the only possible chance was to run the massive club suit and hope for something to develop. With one club to go, and Mbozi already under pressure in the West seat, these cards were still alive:

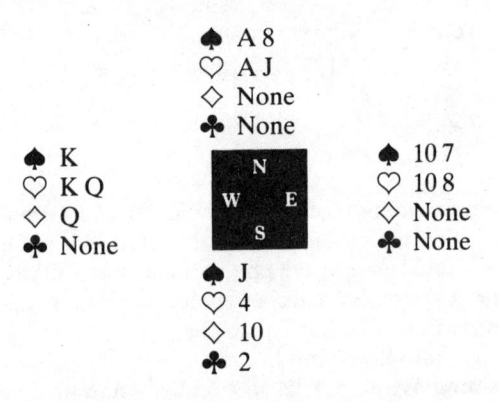

On the last club Mbozi threw the king of spades, but now Brother Tobias could cash the spade knave and enter dummy with a heart to make the ace of spades.

"For a moment you had me puzzled," said Brother Tobias, reaching for his scorepad. "Rather a pretty ending, wasn't it?"

"You could hardly be goin' wrong with me holdin' all de six

picture cards," replied Mbozi moodily. "Even if you barin' de spade ace, contract is still makin'."

"What nonsense, Mbozi!" cried Brother Tobias. "I've been playing bridge for thirty years. What do you think you can tell me about the game after just three months? Look, I'll show you. If I bare the ace, this would be the ending...."

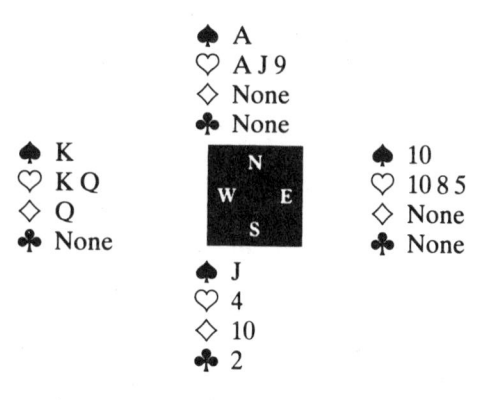

♠ A
♡ A J 9
◇ None
♣ None

♠ K   ♠ 10
♡ K Q   ♡ 10 8 5
◇ Q   ◇ None
♣ None   ♣ None

♠ J
♡ 4
◇ 10
♣ 2

"Now on the last club you simply throw a spade," he said. "Is that too difficult?"

"Oh, yes. I see, bwana," replied Mbozi humbly. "But what if you throw de spade ace from dummy and then play de jack of spades. What do I do then?"

Brother Tobias blinked a couple of times and then swept up the cards in his huge hands.

"I can't waste any more time following up your absurd suggestions," he said fiercely. "Now, what does the rubber come to?"

"Any luck with de wild pigs?" asked Mbozi, later that evening.

"No. Wasted best part of de afternoon tryin' to track 'em," replied Mjubu. "How was de bridge game?"

"Didn't give me a single glass of whisky-drink all afternoon," said Mbozi sullenly. "Apparently seems you don't get any if you criticise de white bwanas' play."

Into Zbolwumba Territory

"Brother Luke, the time has arrived for us to take our courage in our hands," said Brother Tobias, looking rather pale.

"Oh? What do you mean exactly?"

"We must send a visiting party to the Zbolwumba tribe and try to convert them to Acol, just as we have done here so successfully."

Brother Luke expressed his doubts on the matter with a low whistle. "Do you think that's wise?" he said. "After all, it's less than four years since Brothers Trappitus and Bernard played a rather tragic role in one of their barbecues."

"Brother Luke, we were not sent here just to acquire a suntan," reprimanded Brother Tobias. "Surely you don't want to condemn the Zbolwumbas to a lifetime of playing their abominable relay system?"

The visiting party was soon made up. Accompanying the two missionaries would be Mjubu, the owner of the elephant that would transport them, Mbozi who would act as interpreter, and the witch-doctor, whose presence would undoubtedly add considerable authority to the group. Mjubu's elephant had been fitted out with a specially constructed howdah, on which the four passengers could sit facing each other and so enjoy a game while the long journey was in progress.

Love all, dealer South

```
              ♠ Q 7 5
              ♡ A 6
              ◇ 8 7 2
              ♣ Q 10 8 6 4
♠ K 8 6 2                      ♠ J 10 3
♡ Q 10 7 3     N              ♡ J 8 5 2
◇ 6 4 3      W   E            ◇ J 10 9
♣ 9 3          S              ♣ A 7 5
              ♠ A 9 4
              ♡ K 9 4
              ◇ A K Q 5
              ♣ K J 2
```

S	W	N	E
Bro.	Bro.	Witch-	
Tobias	Luke	doctor	Mbozi
1 ♣	No	4 ♣	No
4 NT	No	5 ♢	No
6 ♣	End		

Judging his hand to be somewhat thin for a 2 NT opening, Brother Tobias opened the auction with one club. The witch-doctor, who always employed a rather optimistic version of the losing trick count, raised him exuberantly to the four-level. Brother Tobias discovered there was an ace missing and decided it would be safer to bid the small slam in clubs. The witch-doctor surely had five clubs for his raise, otherwise he would have attempted to play the hand.

Brother Luke led the three of hearts and the witch-doctor tabled his cards.

"I regularly always takin' off one loser for havin' de fifth trump," he explained to his bewildered partner. "I readin' dis in one of de books in your hut."

"If the book recommended raises to the four-level on that rubbish," replied Brother Tobias severely, "remind me to burn it when we get back."

At this moment the elephant trod on one of the upturned spikes planted by the Zbolwumba scouts and let out a trumpet of protest.

"*If* we get back," said Brother Luke.

The heart lead ran to the knave and king and declarer played on trumps immediately. Mbozi won the first round and, instead of dislodging the ace of hearts, returned the knave of diamonds, a play that left the contract with one spark of life.

Brother Tobias played off the entire trump suit, discarding two spades from hand, then cashed his diamond honours. The thirteenth diamond was led in the end-position shown overleaf.

West discarded a heart, hoping that his partner held the nine. Brother Tobias then cashed the ace of hearts, ace of spades and nine of hearts for his contract.

"I hope you all followed how I played that," he exclaimed proudly. "If I'm not mistaken that was a genuine cr . . . aargh!"

A low-hanging branch almost knocked him off the elephant. Despite frequent warnings Mjubu took great delight in steering the

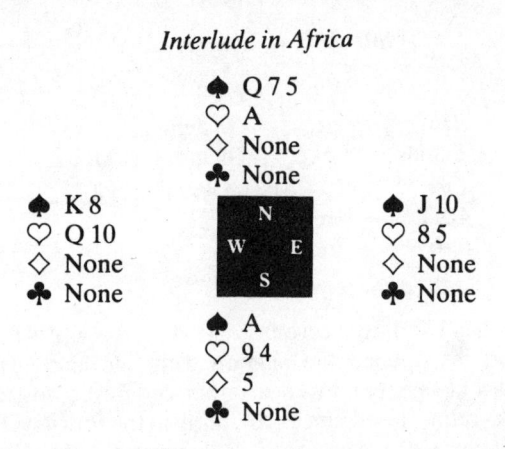

♠ Q 7 5
♡ A
◇ None
♣ None

♠ K 8   ♠ J 10
♡ Q 10   ♡ 8 5
◇ None   ◇ None
♣ None   ♣ None

♠ A
♡ 9 4
◇ 5
♣ None

elephant into such hazards when his passengers' attention seemed to be elsewhere.

"Most sorry, bwana," said Mjubu, rocking with laughter. "I tell him go left, but he some reason go right."

In what proved to be the last hand before they reached the Zbolwumba settlement, the cards were dealt as follows:

E–W game, dealer East

♠ K 8
♡ J 9 7 2
◇ K 6 2
♣ A Q J 5

♠ 10 6 5 4 3   ♠ A Q J 9
♡ 10   ♡ A 8 6
◇ 10 9 8 7 5   ◇ A
♣ 6 4   ♣ 10 9 7 3 2

♠ 7 2
♡ K Q 5 4 3
◇ Q J 4 3
♣ K 8

S	W	N	E
Bro.	Witch-		Bro.
Luke	doctor	Mbozi	Tobias
			1 ♣
1 ♡	No	4 ♡	End

The witch-doctor led the ten of diamonds and Brother Tobias

won with his singleton ace. It seemed that declarer was destined to succeed, having escaped a spade lead. Surely he had four trump tricks, four club tricks and at least two diamonds to take. With a sigh Brother Tobias pulled out the ten of clubs but, at the last possible moment, he noticed quite a reasonable chance of defeating the contract. If his partner had the spade ten it could be transformed into an entry for a diamond ruff. Pushing the futile ten of clubs back where it belonged, Brother Tobias switched to the queen of spades, which was captured on the table.

Declarer placed East with the singleton diamond ace after this play, but saw there was little future in going for a quick discard on the clubs. If West did have as many as three clubs, East would have a 4–4–1–4 distribution and with two sure trump tricks he would obviously have taken his ace of spades at trick 2.

Instead declarer tried to slip through a round of trumps, but Brother Tobias whipped in with his ace and followed it with the nine of spades. He was disturbed to see the witch-doctor, sitting West, give this card a long look, apparently unsure whether he should overtake it.

"Hah, hah! I'm not dat stupid, bwana," said the witch-doctor eventually, overtaking the spade and returning a diamond. "I just findin' it amusin' to make you sweat a bit."

"Look out, bwana! Zbolwumbas!" cried Mjubu, as a group of hostile natives ran out of a thicket towards the elephant.

"Right, Mbozi," said Brother Tobias urgently. "Tell them that we bring news of a wonderful bidding system based on limit bids and a 12–14 no-trump."

"Zbolwumban!" cried Mbozi. "M'hat jumbura lo Acol sbarada ca'hem limdzaba azohan al 12–14 s'hen-attot."

"Boggazut!" shouted the largest of the natives, pulling the two missionaries violently to the ground. "Ngem 12–14 s'hen-attot dozar f'haram 800 ob 1100!"

The imposing figure of the local chieftain came forward, silencing the gathering with an imperious wave of his fly-switch.

"Good evening, white-bwana," he said, eyeing the capacious frame of Brother Tobias approvingly. "I most pleased to see you."

"Ah, you speak English," replied Brother Tobias, struggling to his feet. "That's a most promising start."

"Not so much pleased with other white-bwana," added the chieftain, casting a practised eye over Brother Luke. "He bit on de skinny side."

PART III

Return to the Monastery

22

Brother Paulo's Riposte

Thursday night at the Monastery of St. Titus was duplicate night. The Abbot, who by tradition always sat North at table five near the fire, did not take part in the draw for starting positions. He considered it undignified for him to have to move between rounds. Nor was he willing to expose his health to the notoriously draughty tables eleven and twelve near the door.

Tonight was a somewhat special occasion because it was the first appearance of Brother Paulo, recently signed from the Monastery of San Giovanni Battista, near Milan. The Abbot had been looking forward all week to tonight's game, but judging from his sour expression it appeared that one or two unpleasant entries must have already found their way on to his scorecard.

Love all, dealer West

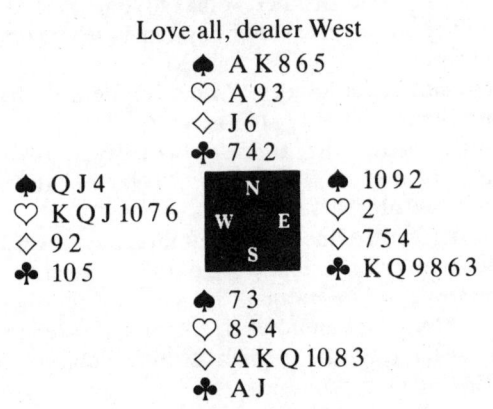

```
                    ♠ A K 8 6 5
                    ♡ A 9 3
                    ◇ J 6
                    ♣ 7 4 2
    ♠ Q J 4                        ♠ 10 9 2
    ♡ K Q J 10 7 6      N          ♡ 2
    ◇ 9 2           W     E        ◇ 7 5 4
    ♣ 10 5              S          ♣ K Q 9 8 6 3
                    ♠ 7 3
                    ♡ 8 5 4
                    ◇ A K Q 10 8 3
                    ♣ A J
```

Brother Paulo's Riposte

S	W	N	E
Bro.	Bro.	The	Bro.
Paulo	Fabius	Abbot	Aelred
	2 ♡[1]	2 ♠	No
4 ◇	No	5 ◇	End

[1] A weak two bid, 6 to 10 points.

The king of hearts was led and Brother Paulo, reputedly a fine player of the cards, inspected the dummy carefully. One possible line was to draw trumps and exit with a heart. If West feebly cashed another heart, declarer might be able to squeeze East in the black suits.

Another plan was to draw trumps and play a spade to the eight if West followed small. This required the combination of West being asleep and spades being 3–3.

Brother Paulo sneaked a quick glance at Brother Fabius, sitting West. Unfortunately he looked far too sharp-eyed to allow either of these plays to succeed. Surely declarer's hopes lay with East, who was looking vacantly round the room. Brother Paulo accordingly ducked the opening lead and put up the ace at trick 2 when hearts were continued.

The Abbot, who had shown some concern when the ace of hearts was not played at the first trick, raised his eyes in horrified disbelief as East now ruffed the ace into oblivion. To think that Brother Paulo had been specially recommended by Cardinal Montaglio!

When declarer won the club return, ruffed the spades good, drew trumps ending in dummy and claimed the contract, the Abbot's expression changed in a flash to one of knowledgeable approval.

"Cleverly played, Brother Paulo," he said. "I was hoping you would spot that play."

"Yes, if East is not er . . . tromping the ace, I am finished."

"No need to look so sad, Brother Aelred," remarked the Abbot, unfolding the travelling scoresheet. "Brother Paulo and I have played the game before, you know, and . . ."

His voice faded away.

"Another bottom for us, is it?" enquired Brother Paulo, picking up the scoresheet, which had slipped through the Abbot's disbelieving fingers. "Yes, just as I thought. Three no-trumps 430, two hearts with double 500. 500? Ah yes, North is refusing to overtromp the diamond, and South is then er . . . uppercutting the fourth round of

spades. Even two pairs are bidding game in spades. What is our pair number, Abbot?"

"Five," murmured the Abbot, gazing pensively into the fire. Suddenly he thought he understood why his predecessor, the Abbot LeStrange, had introduced bridge to the monastery so many years ago. What finer discipline could there be than learning to accept without complaint the – how did it go? – the slings and arrows of outrageous fortune. With an effort he conjured up a glassy smile.

"What an instructive hand that was!" he said.

To the Abbot's considerable relief, the tide of ill-fortune that had besieged table five all evening began to recede. A succession of part-score hands provided some fertile territory for their superior cardplay, and with one round to go the Abbot and Brother Paulo had every chance of achieving a respectable position.

"I can't understand it," frowned the Abbot. "Lucius and Xavier are coming to our table. I'm sure I told Brother Zac to fix the movement so that we wouldn't have to play against them."

"They won't bother us, Abbot," replied Brother Paulo, scratching his chin confidently. "We end with two big ones. You wait and see."

"Oh hello, Lucius. Lovely to see you," beamed the Abbot. "I told Brother Zac to arrange the movement so that we would meet in the last round. How are you doing?"

"A little above average, perhaps," replied Brother Lucius.

That's what he always says, thought the Abbot crossly. Why can't he admit when he's been lucky?

Love all, dealer West

```
              ♠ A K 9 7
              ♡ Q 3
              ◇ K J 9 8 5 2
              ♣ 6
 ♠ 3                          ♠ Q 10 6 4
 ♡ K 10 9 7 5      N          ♡ J 8 6 2
 ◇ 4          W        E      ◇ A 7
 ♣ J 8 7 4 3 2     S          ♣ A Q 9
              ♠ J 8 5 2
              ♡ A 4
              ◇ Q 10 6 3
              ♣ K 10 5
```

Brother Paulo's Riposte

S	W	N	E
Bro.	Bro.	The	Bro.
Paulo	Xavier	Abbot	Lucius
	No	1 ◇	dble
1 ♠	4 ♡	4 ♠	dble

Brother Lucius doubled the Abbot's diamond opening and Brother Paulo, who believed in ignoring the double, replied one spade. When West leapt to four hearts, the Abbot, expecting his partner to hold a better suit, bid the spade game. East's double closed the auction.

The ten of hearts was led and captured by dummy's queen. It seemed likely from East's voluble contribution to the auction that he had at least four trumps and both the missing aces. Brother Paulo began to play out the hand in his mind. If he played ace, king and another spade, East would win and knock out the heart ace. Declarer would not be able to draw the last trump until he had forced out the ace of diamonds. When East took the ace he would doubtless force the dummy with a third round of hearts, and there would be no entry to hand to pull the last trump.

Suddenly an elegant solution to the problem flashed into his mind.

"Ace of tromps," he requested, noting with approval that West followed.

"Nine of tromps," he continued, in a confident tone.

East won and knocked out the heart ace as expected, but when he took the second round of diamonds and returned a heart, Brother Paulo was able to ruff with dummy's king and draw trumps by finessing the eight.

"Well played, Brother Paulo," said the Abbot. "I was hoping you would see the advantage of underleading the king of trumps. Er . . . what does that come to, Lucius? 590, is it?"

"That's right, Abbot," replied Brother Lucius unconcernedly. "I noticed a couple of 590s on the scoresheet for board 3. Quite a popular score tonight."

The Abbot glanced at his scorecard. Yes, typical of Lucius to have noticed that result.

With a pointed clearing of his throat Brother Paulo drew the Abbot's attention to the fact that there was still one board to play.

N–S game, dealer East

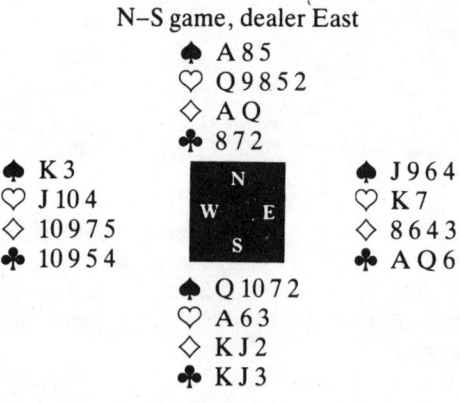

```
                         ♠ A 8 5
                         ♡ Q 9 8 5 2
                         ◇ A Q
                         ♣ 8 7 2
        ♠ K 3                              ♠ J 9 6 4
        ♡ J 10 4                           ♡ K 7
        ◇ 10 9 7 5                         ◇ 8 6 4 3
        ♣ 10 9 5 4                         ♣ A Q 6
                         ♠ Q 10 7 2
                         ♡ A 6 3
                         ◇ K J 2
                         ♣ K J 3
```

Determined to press home his advantage, Brother Paulo opened one heart on the South cards, intending to rebid in no-trumps. The Abbot, sitting North, glanced anxiously to his left while considering his reply. No one had a keener nose for sacrifices than Brother Lucius. Some preventative action was called for.

"One spade," replied the Abbot in a loud voice.

Brother Paulo raised him to two spades and now the Abbot bid four hearts. Brother Paulo looked pained at this unfavourable development. Had the Abbot never heard of a tactical opening bid? Never mind, there was a simple remedy at hand.

"Four spades," he declared in a tone of finality.

The Abbot sent a headmasterly glare winging across the table. Had these Italians never heard of a tactical response? His bid of five hearts concluded the auction.

S	W	N	E
Bro.	Bro.	The	Bro.
Paulo	Xavier	Abbot	Lucius
			No
1 ♡	No	1 ♠	No
2 ♠	No	4 ♡	No
4 ♠	No	5 ♡	End

The ten of diamonds was led and the Abbot revealed his embarrassing dummy. There seemed to Brother Paulo to be only one slim chance. He would need both club honours onside and an endplay. He won the diamond in dummy and led a small club,

winning with the knave when East followed small. Returning to dummy with a diamond, he led a second club, taken by East's ace.

The club return was captured by the king. Brother Paulo discarded a spade on the king of diamonds and threw East in with ace and another trump, ducking in dummy. These cards remained:

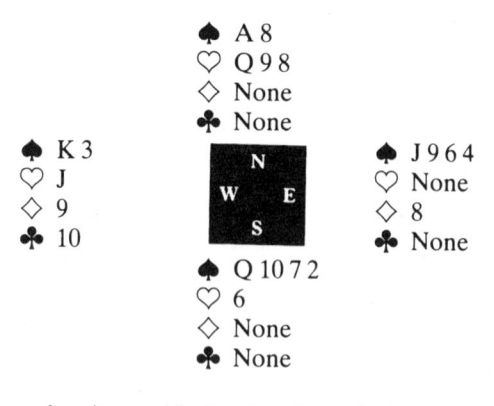

♠ A 8
♡ Q 9 8
◇ None
♣ None

♠ K 3   ♠ J 9 6 4
♡ J   ♡ None
◇ 9   ◇ 8
♣ 10   ♣ None

♠ Q 10 7 2
♡ 6
◇ None
♣ None

A diamond exit would clearly allow declarer to spirit away dummy's spade loser, so Brother Lucius returned a spade. As East had already shown good values, Brother Paulo inserted the ten. When this forced a reluctant king from West, declarer won with the ace and made eleven tricks.

The Abbot reached gleefully for the travelling scoresheet. "Good gracious!" he exclaimed. "Four pairs went down in four hearts."

"That could be," said Brother Paulo. "Declarer may be starting on the tromps."

"So our delicate auction landed us in the par contract," concluded the Abbot, giving his partner a wicked smile. "Five hearts is cold and four hearts goes one off."

"It's a matter of luck if the opportunity for a clever play presents itself," said Brother Lucius rather stiffly, rising to his feet.

"I am thinking of another clever play," Brother Paulo replied. "Suppose you are dropping the king of hearts under the ace. How am I making eleven tricks then?"

Safer in a Slam

"I thought you said this team was hopeless, Abbot," said Brother Xavier with a worried glance at his scorecard.

"Perhaps I did. With two women in their team, I naturally assumed that . . ."

"If I remember rightly," persisted Brother Lucius, "you told us this would make a good practice match for the next round."

"There's no need to go on about it," replied the Abbot testily. "If you hadn't bid that absurd spade slam we'd be practically level anyway. Everyone just play straight down the middle in the last set and we can still win."

Board 28. N–S game, dealer West

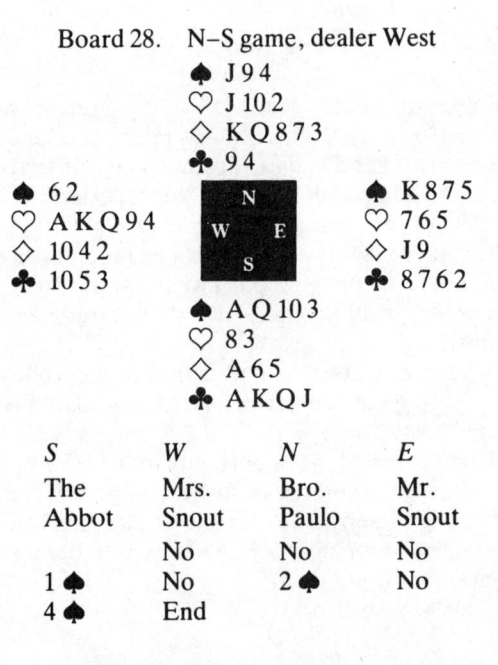

```
                    ♠ J 9 4
                    ♡ J 10 2
                    ◇ K Q 8 7 3
                    ♣ 9 4
   ♠ 6 2                          ♠ K 8 7 5
   ♡ A K Q 9 4         N          ♡ 7 6 5
   ◇ 10 4 2        W       E      ◇ J 9
   ♣ 10 5 3           S          ♣ 8 7 6 2
                    ♠ A Q 10 3
                    ♡ 8 3
                    ◇ A 6 5
                    ♣ A K Q J
```

S	W	N	E
The	Mrs.	Bro.	Mr.
Abbot	Snout	Paulo	Snout
	No	No	No
1 ♣	No	2 ♠	No
4 ♠	End		

Mrs. Snout began with three top hearts and the Abbot, with a knowledgeable air, discarded a small diamond. Since West had been unable to open the bidding it was reasonable to place the spade

king onside. By discarding on the third trick, the Abbot planned to keep control of the hand if East had four trumps.

"Having no tromps?" asked Brother Paulo.

"That may be quite a passable joke by Italian standards," retorted the Abbot. "In England our jokes tend to be a good deal sharper than that."

The Abbot's merriment was cut short when Mrs. Snout continued unexpectedly with a fourth round of hearts. The Abbot paused. Had he miscalculated? To ruff high in the dummy now might promote a trump trick for the defence, so he ruffed low. Declining to overruff, Mr. Snout discarded the nine of diamonds. After some thought the Abbot threw his ace of diamonds and then ran the knave of trumps, followed by the nine. Since Mr. Snout had not covered the knave of spades, the Abbot was inclined to place him with four trumps. The nine of diamonds discard suggested a short diamond holding. If it was a singleton the contract was doomed, so the Abbot decided to play East for a 4–3–2–4 distribution.

He cashed four rounds of clubs and crossed to the king of diamonds. The lead was in dummy now and his last two cards were the ace and queen of trumps.

"Yes, er . . . well played, Abbot," said Brother Paulo. "Maybe the other room play in no-tromps?"

"Yes," chortled the Abbot. "I wonder what you would have led against 3 NT, Mrs. Snort?"

"The name is Snout," came the sharp reply. "Shall we get on? You were extremely slow on that last hand."

"The play, if I may say so, was far from simple," replied the Abbot with dignity.

"It's very hot in here, Bill," observed Mrs. Snout, fanning herself with her scorecard. "Can you open a window or something?"

"Yes, of course, my love," said Mr. Snout, leaping obediently to his feet. "Perhaps I could get you a cold drink?"

"That's extremely kind of you," interposed the Abbot. "A whisky would go down very nicely. We rarely get the opportunity to sample such luxuries in our walk of life."

In the other room, meanwhile, the monastery pair were ignoring the Abbot's instructions to play down the middle.

Board 31.   N–S game, dealer South

```
            ♠ 9 6 4
            ♡ A K Q 10
            ◇ J 8 5
            ♣ A K 3
♠ K 10 8 5 3            ♠ A 7 2
♡ 5 2          N        ♡ 8 7 6 4
◇ 10 4 2   W     E      ◇ Q 9 6 3
♣ 8 7 6        S        ♣ 5 2
            ♠ Q J
            ♡ J 9 3
            ◇ A K 7
            ♣ Q J 10 9 4
```

S	W	N	E
Bro.	Mrs.	Bro.	Mr.
Lucius	Pringle	Xavier	Pringle
1 NT	No	6 NT	End

Adding a point for his handsome club suit and subtracting none for his unsupported spade honours, Brother Lucius opened a fragile 15–17 no-trump. Not to be outdone, Brother Xavier also added a point or two, leaping straight to 6 NT. Mrs. Pringle opted for the safe lead of the eight of clubs and down went the dummy.

"Thank you, partner!" beamed Brother Lucius, sounding as if he wished they were in the grand. "Ace, please!"

One possible plan was to give up a spade immediately and hope that a spade–diamond squeeze would develop, but Brother Lucius rejected this line. Apart from the obvious risk that the defenders might see their way to cashing several spades, the squeeze would work only if East held the diamond queen. In that case a different line of play held more appeal.

Brother Lucius cashed the club suit, the ace of diamonds, and finally the hearts. When he called for the last heart from dummy, this was the end position:

Safer in a Slam

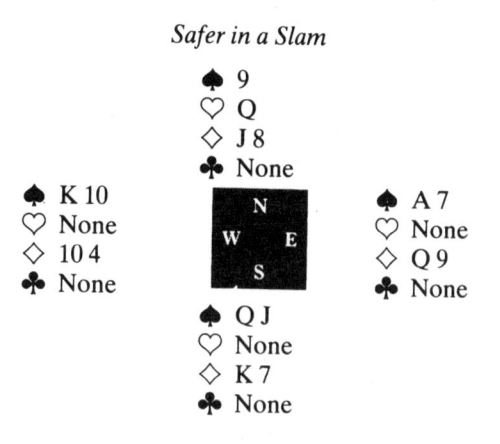

```
              ♠ 9
              ♡ Q
              ◇ J 8
              ♣ None
♠ K 10                        ♠ A 7
♡ None          N             ♡ None
◇ 10 4      W       E         ◇ Q 9
♣ None          S             ♣ None
              ♠ Q J
              ♡ None
              ◇ K 7
              ♣ None
```

Mr. Pringle, in the East seat, ran an index finger nervously across his brown moustache. He obviously couldn't afford a diamond and if he discarded the spade ace declarer would in fact be able to establish a spade trick. Anyway, Mr. Pringle would never dare throw an ace away. His wife did not approve of flashy plays, whatever the result. He therefore parted with a low spade, only to find himself thrown in on the next trick to lead away from his queen of diamonds.

"Oh, Harry. You're always letting that happen to you," complained Mrs. Pringle.

Mr. Pringle blinked. How typical of her to blame him, when it was all her fault for not leading a spade.

"Yes. Sorry, dear," he replied.

"Have you held the fort?" asked the Abbot, when his team-mates arrived to compare scores.

"Well, one or two not so bad," replied Brother Lucius, taking a vacant seat and opening his scorecard.

"What did you do on board 31?" demanded the Abbot. "Did you stay out of no-trumps?"

"No, I'm afraid not, Abbot. That was my fault," said Brother Lucius, casting his eyes apologetically downwards.

"I thought we'd gain on that hand at least," observed the Abbot, shaking his head. "Five clubs was on, not to mention five hearts. You were minus 100, I suppose?"

"No, plus 1440," said Brother Lucius casually. "The no-trump game looked a bit risky, so we decided to play safely in the slam."

The Urgent Message

Brother Aelred and Brother Michael often attended the weekly sale at Dodds & Dodds (Auctioneers) Ltd. Their favourite game was to see how many bids they could make without actually buying anything. The scoring was simple, one point scored for each bid made, but ten points lost for any item actually knocked down to them.

"Lot number 69, nice box of sundry alarm clocks. £5, anyone?" called the auctioneer hopefully. "Ten clocks, some needing attention, bargain here for someone. £4? OK, start me then."

"20p!" said Brother Michael, marking up his scorecard.

"20p bid. Ha! ha! Very amusing! And 30p at the back."

Brother Aelred shot up his hand.

"40p at the front. 40p. At 40p then. I'm selling. Any more? Sold! 40p to you, sir, and the name is Brother er . . .?"

"Aelred," came the sheepish reply. What on earth was he supposed to do with ten broken alarm clocks?

"Ah yes, Brother Aelred. I remember," said the auctioneer heartily. "You're the gentleman who bought the crate of pipe-cleaners, aren't you? I'll put the two lots together."

Brother Aelred followed much the same approach at the bridge table. Whenever he judged he could make a low-level overcall without actually getting doubled, he would do so. His J x x x x overcalls often resulted in an expensive phantom sacrifice or attracted a disastrous K x lead, but his memory seemed immune to such occasions.

"Why in heaven's name did you sacrifice, partner?" Brother Aelred would say. "I had three trump tricks and an ace to take against four hearts. The only reason I overcalled was to try to push them into game."

Brother Aelred deposited the alarm clocks in his cell and walked along the top floor of the monastery's east wing towards the cardroom. He pushed open the brass-studded oak door and surveyed the tables timidly, searching for a low-stake game where he might enjoy a few quiet rubbers.

"Ah, Brother Aelred! We need a fourth over here," boomed a heavy voice from across the cardroom.

Brother Aelred looked over to see three of the most feared cardplayers in the monastery – the Abbot, Brother Lucius and Brother Xavier, the monastery barber.

"No, no, Abbot! I wasn't looking for a game. I'm trying to find Brother Michael. I have an urgent message for him and . . ."

"It can wait," interrupted the Abbot. "Cut for partners."

The early exchanges were even. Then Brother Aelred dealt the following layout:

Game all, dealer South

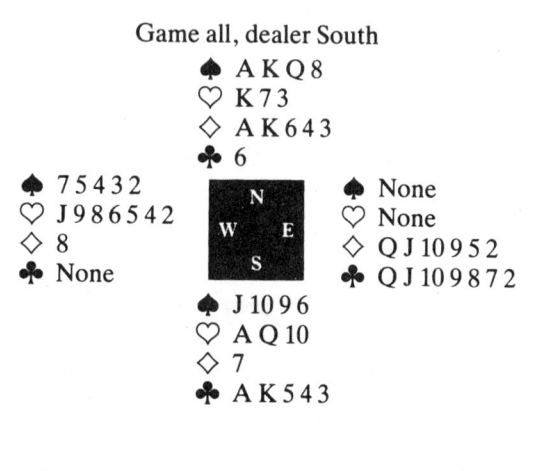

```
              ♠ A K Q 8
              ♡ K 7 3
              ♢ A K 6 4 3
              ♣ 6
♠ 7 5 4 3 2                    ♠ None
♡ J 9 8 6 5 4 2               ♡ None
♢ 8                           ♢ Q J 10 9 5 2
♣ None                        ♣ Q J 10 9 8 7 2
              ♠ J 10 9 6
              ♡ A Q 10
              ♢ 7
              ♣ A K 5 4 3
```

S	W	N	E
Bro.	Bro.	The	Bro.
Aelred	Xavier	Abbot	Lucius
1 ♣	No	1 ♢	No
2 ♣	No	2 ♠	No
3 NT	No	6 NT	dble

When the auction unexpectedly vaulted to the six-level, Brother Lucius, sitting East, could scarcely believe his good fortune. With every suit breaking badly and Brother Aelred as declarer, he would shortly be inscribing 800 or more above the line.

"Double," he said, in a diffident tone that belied his thoughts.

All passed and Brother Xavier led his singleton diamond.

"With anyone else I would redouble," muttered the Abbot as he put down the dummy.

Brother Aelred glanced at his cards and suddenly his heart missed a beat. Nestling like a viper in the middle of his six-card club suit was

the six of spades. He looked aghast at the horrible pointed symbols all over the offending card.

A chilling implication of his mistake flashed into his mind. He had failed to raise one of the Abbot's suits. The last monk to try that trick was ... what was his name? Oh yes, old Brother Bernard. What on earth had happened to him? Brother Aelred wondered sadly. No one had heard of him since.

Determined to delay his exposure as long as possible, he left the six of spades concealed in the middle of his club suit and began to cash some of his winners. After three rounds of hearts he played the ace-king of spades following with the 9 and 10 from hand. When the spade queen was led to trick 7, the position was as follows:

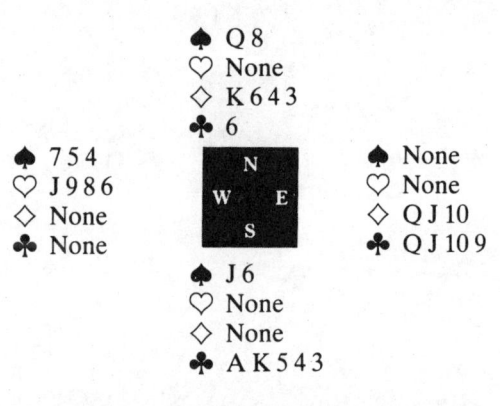

♠ Q 8
♡ None
♢ K 6 4 3
♣ 6

♠ 7 5 4
♡ J 9 8 6
♢ None
♣ None

♠ None
♡ None
♢ Q J 10
♣ Q J 10 9

♠ J 6
♡ None
♢ None
♣ A K 5 4 3

East discarded the knave of diamonds and declarer followed with knave of spades. An intriguing thought now occurred to Brother Aelred. Maybe in some way he had performed a squeeze, and those diamonds lying on the table were all good. Hoping for the best, he played king and another diamond. When East won and exited with a club, Brother Aelred took his ace-king of clubs and shamefacedly produced the six of spades, conceding two down.

"On the contrary, Brother Aelred," gloated the Abbot. "The dummy is indisputably high. A variation of the see-saw squeeze, I fancy. But ... er ... you seem to have held FOUR spades."

"Yes, well, you see," said Brother Aelred, "I had A Q 10 of hearts and I sensed that the spades might be breaking badly." He had heard other players use this phrase and hoped that the explanation would be accepted.

"Hmm," said the Abbot heavily. Well, he'd won a good rubber

and nothing would be gained by pressing the matter. "I make the rubber 18. Now you'd better find Brother Whatsisname and give him that message."

"I won't break up your game, Abbot," Brother Aelred replied. "It wasn't such an important message. I've got time for one more rubber."

"Very well, but this will have to be my last. I have to make some notes for my sermon at evensong."

Game all, dealer South

```
                    ♠ 7 5
                    ♡ A 4
                    ◇ A K J 7
                    ♣ K J 10 6 5
  ♠ A Q J 10 9 2                    ♠ 6 3
  ♡ K Q              N              ♡ J 10 9 7 5 2
  ◇ 9 8 2        W       E          ◇ Q 10 5 3
  ♣ 7 4              S              ♣ 3
                    ♠ K 8 4
                    ♡ 8 6 3
                    ◇ 6 4
                    ♣ A Q 9 8 2
```

S	W	N	E
Bro.	The	Bro.	Bro.
Xavier	Abbot	Aelred	Lucius
No	1 ♠	2 NT	No
4 ♣	No	5 ♣	End

Brother Aelred had made a study of the 2 NT overcall and was happy to display his expertise. "I hope this is all right," he said as he put down the dummy after the lead of the heart king. "I've only nine cards in the minors as you can see, but with so many points I . . ."

"Yes, yes. Most excellent bidding," said Brother Xavier dismissively, more interested in trying to uncover a reasonable line of play.

The diamond finesse might well be right, but one discard would not help. What if West had queen to four diamonds and the spade ace? Yes. Duck the king of hearts, and later ruff a heart and run the trump suit. West would have to bare the spade ace to keep the

diamonds guarded, and then a spade could be conceded to establish the king.

"I might have doubled instead," Brother Aelred persisted, "but my hearts were under strength and . . ."

"Two no-trumps was fine," said Brother Xavier impatiently. "Now please, a moment's quiet while I plan the play."

Another chance was to find West with king-queen or king-queen-knave bare in hearts and the queen of diamonds; then he could be endplayed after a heart had been discarded on a top diamond. Yes, this was surely the best chance.

When the ace of hearts was played East signalled with the knave, so Brother Xavier decided to play West for king-queen alone. In this case the diamond finesse, for a heart discard, would not be needed.

Two rounds of trumps were quickly followed by ace, king and another diamond. Brother Lucius, in the East seat, was most interested to see declarer spurn the diamond finesse. It could only mean that he had a 3–3–2–5 distribution and no interest in a discard.

On the third round of diamonds, therefore, Brother Lucius contributed the queen. Declarer ruffed and crossed back with a trump to extract West's last diamond. When the diamond ten appeared on his right instead, declarer gasped with amazement. He ruffed and the Abbot hastily discarded the queen of hearts. A few seconds later the hand was over.

Brother Xavier began to congratulate Brother Lucius on his play of the queen of diamonds, but he was interrupted by the Abbot.

"Did you observe my discard of the heart queen?" he demanded. "The old fox has not entirely lost his cunning. Now I regret I must cut the rubber short and retire to my cell for a couple of hours' meditation before evensong. Would one of you be so kind as to give me a knock at six o'clock?"

"Oh, there's no need for that, Abbot," said Brother Aelred. "Let me lend you an alarm clock. I'm sure I can find a spare one in my cell somewhere."

The Redemption of Brother Sextus

The monastery individual championship was traditionally played over two consecutive Thursdays during Lent. This year the Abbot had fortified his own chances by bringing the event forward to some dates when Brother Lucius would be away from the monastery, lecturing at a seminar on tax avoidance.

This had not, however, deterred Brother Lucius from running his usual discreet book on the event. Those interested were being offered: 9/2 PAULO, 5 ABBOT, 13/2 XAVIER, 9 FABIUS, DAMIEN, 12/1 BAR.

After the first evening most of the favourites were handily placed, and there was keen anticipation when the second day began.

Game all, dealer South

```
                    ♠ K 8 6 5
                    ♡ J 4 2
                    ♢ 7 6 2
                    ♣ 8 5 3
    ♠ 10 9 4 3            N            ♠ J 7 2
    ♡ Q 9 5                            ♡ K 10 6 3
    ♢ 5          W         E           ♢ J 10 9 8 3
    ♣ Q J 10 9 4        S              ♣ 7
                    ♠ A Q
                    ♡ A 8 7
                    ♢ A K Q 4
                    ♣ A K 6 2
```

S	W	N	E
The	Bro.	Bro.	Bro.
Abbot	Sextus	Paulo	Zac
2 ♣	No	2 ♢	No
3 NT	End		

Brother Sextus led the queen of clubs and continued the suit when the Abbot ducked. East discarded a diamond on the second trick and the Abbot, winning in hand, tapped his pencil thoughtfully on the table. Unless West held both heart honours it would be

possible to duck two rounds of hearts safely, rectifying the count. Then, provided the opponents had not been unexpectedly active in the spade suit, a ninth trick could surely be conjured up in the endgame. At least one defender would have to keep three spades and this player would be exposed to a throw-in.

The Abbot put down his pencil and set his plan in action by leading a small heart. Fearing that declarer might hold A K x x, West put up the queen of hearts and exited with a further high club to declarer's ace, East discarding a spade. Since one diamond had been discarded, the Abbot played off two top diamonds before risking a second heart. As expected, West discarded on the second round.

When West played low on the next round of hearts the Abbot glanced sharply at his partner, to make sure that Brother Paulo was following the play. East returned the ten of hearts and these cards were left:

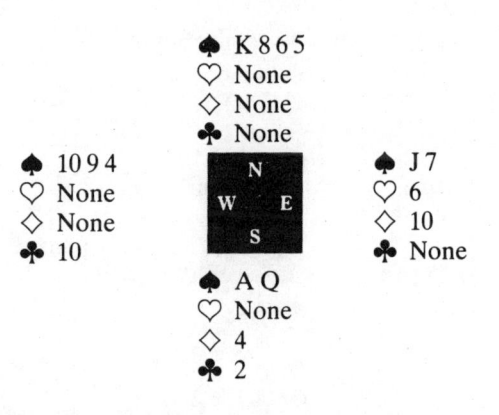

Only one spade had been discarded, so there was no future in overtaking the spade queen. Brother Zac's retention of the thirteenth heart had annoyingly denied the Abbot a complete count on the hand. After cashing the ♠ A Q he was faced with an unpleasant guess. Should he exit with a club, playing West for the outstanding spade, or with a diamond, to endplay East?

"It hardly affects the outcome of the hand, Brother Zac," said the Abbot playfully, "but I was just wondering ... are your last two cards the same colour?"

"I've no idea, Abbot," replied Brother Zac impassively. "I've been colour-blind since birth, I'm afraid. Runs in my family."

On a sudden impulse the Abbot tried his luck with a club, and the game was home. "A stepping-stone squeeze," remarked the Abbot carelessly, wiping the sweat from his brow. "They don't turn up so often."

"Aha, a well-deserving top for you, Abbot," congratulated Brother Paulo. "And, of course, one for me."

The Abbot's smile evaporated. Why couldn't this hand have arrived when he was playing *against* Brother Paulo? In accordance with the movement, the players changed partners for the next hand.

N–S game, dealer South

```
              ♠ A 9 6
              ♡ 5 4
              ◇ A 7 4 2
              ♣ Q 7 6 4
  ♠ 10 7 3         N         ♠ J 8 5 4 2
  ♡ K Q 10 8 3  W     E      ♡ 9 7
  ◇ 8              S         ◇ 10 9 3
  ♣ K 10 5 2                 ♣ J 9 3
              ♠ K Q
              ♡ A J 6 2
              ◇ K Q J 6 5
              ♣ A 8
```

S	W	N	E
Bro.	The	Bro.	Bro.
Paulo	Abbot	Zac	Sextus
1 ◇	1 ♡	3 ◇	No
4 NT	No	5 ♡	No
6 ◇	End		

The Abbot, disappointed to find his main rival at the helm in a slam, chose the king of hearts for his opening lead.

"Small, please!" requested Brother Paulo, who was renowned for his lightning-quick cardplay. He won the first trick in hand, East petering with the nine, then played the K Q of trumps, followed by the K Q of spades. Since the approaching discard on the spade ace would have to be a club, Brother Paulo also cashed the ace of clubs before crossing to the table's ace of trumps. When the spade ace was called for, these cards remained:

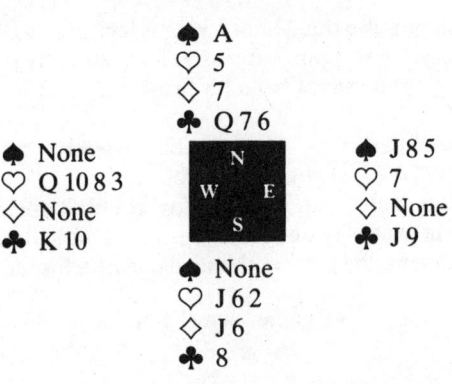

```
              ♠ A
              ♡ 5
              ◇ 7
              ♣ Q 7 6
   ♠ None                    ♠ J 8 5
   ♡ Q 10 8 3        N       ♡ 7
   ◇ None        W       E   ◇ None
   ♣ K 10           S       ♣ J 9
              ♠ None
              ♡ J 6 2
              ◇ J 6
              ♣ 8
```

Declarer threw his club and the Abbot had no good discard. A club would allow his king to be ruffed out, and if he threw a heart, either the 3 or the 8, he would be exposed to an endplay. Finally he discarded the three of hearts.

"Small heart!" said Brother Paulo, awaiting East's discard with interest. When the seven came, he ducked; the Abbot had to overtake and give him a trick on the return.

"You've cost us a top, partner!" cried the Abbot in anguish. "Why did you play your nine on the first trick?"

"The nine of hearts? Well, I had a doubleton," replied Brother Sextus, looking mystified.

"If you keep the nine," persisted the Abbot, "I can underplay it with my eight when declarer doesn't cover."

"Well, one top wouldn't make much difference to my score," replied Brother Sextus, studying his card. "I was more than two tops below average after the first session and I haven't improved much."

The Abbot blinked in disbelief. How had someone with such a singularly selfish outlook ever decided to become a monk?

"Quite so," he said heavily. "I quite understand. That your partner might possibly be concerned in the outcome is of no importance. None whatever."

"Oh dear," apologised Brother Sextus. "From now on I promise you I'll try hard not to let anyone down."

Having switched partnerships, the players took their cards for the final round:

The Redemption of Brother Sextus

E–W game, dealer West

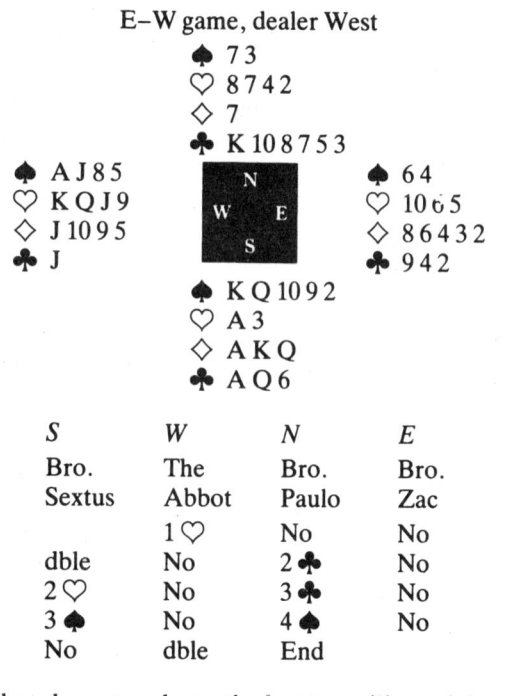

♠ 7 3
♡ 8 7 4 2
♢ 7
♣ K 10 8 7 5 3

♠ A J 8 5
♡ K Q J 9
♢ J 10 9 5
♣ J

♠ 6 4
♡ 10 6 5
♢ 8 6 4 3 2
♣ 9 4 2

♠ K Q 10 9 2
♡ A 3
♢ A K Q
♣ A Q 6

S	W	N	E
Bro.	The	Bro.	Bro.
Sextus	Abbot	Paulo	Zac
	1 ♡	No	No
dble	No	2 ♣	No
2 ♡	No	3 ♣	No
3 ♠	No	4 ♠	No
No	dble	End	

The Abbot, keen to salvage the lost top without delay, doubled and led the king of hearts.

"You won't make this one," said Brother Paulo, as he displayed the dummy and turned to his glass of arrowroot. "Still, you said you were out of the running."

Remembering his recent promise, Brother Sextus spent a full minute considering his line of play. The Abbot, meanwhile, contented himself with a few pointed glances at his watch. Eventually Brother Sextus ducked the first heart, won the second and then cashed his three diamond honours, discarding hearts from the table. His intention was clearly to use dummy's meagre trump holding to counter the Abbot's forcing defence.

The king of trumps at this point would be a mistake. Instead, Brother Sextus led the ten of trumps from hand. The Abbot won with the knave but was now powerless to defeat the contract, since a red suit return could be ruffed on the table.

"Magnifico!" exclaimed Brother Paulo. "You are miracle man."

"I imagine they'll be in the club slam at most tables," remarked

the Abbot, reaching for the score-slip. "I fancy it can be done, even after a heart lead. Discard two spades on the diamonds and so on. What's this? Only one pair in six clubs and they didn't make it?"

"Sabotage!" cried Brother Paulo, winking at his partner.

The Abbot's Wager

"I think Brother Paulo and myself should play against the two women in the last set," whispered the Abbot in a conspiratorial manner. "I seem to make them quite nervous for some reason."

A timid knocking at the half-open door announced the return of the Misses Clutterbuck, so Brother Lucius and Brother Xavier gathered up their scorecards and left the room.

"24 to us, do you make it, ladies?" boomed the Abbot in an intimidating voice.

"Is that what you made it, Ethel? Yes, you're right: 24."

Love all, dealer West

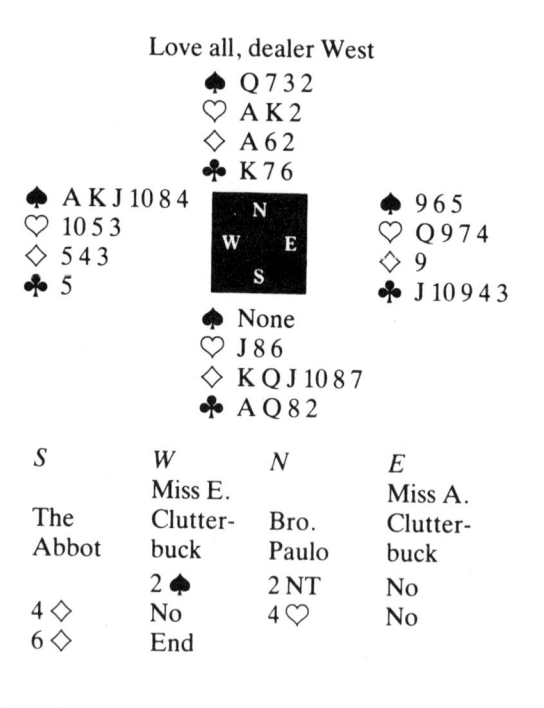

```
              ♠ Q 7 3 2
              ♡ A K 2
              ◇ A 6 2
              ♣ K 7 6
♠ A K J 10 8 4              ♠ 9 6 5
♡ 10 5 3                   ♡ Q 9 7 4
◇ 5 4 3                    ◇ 9
♣ 5                       ♣ J 10 9 4 3
              ♠ None
              ♡ J 8 6
              ◇ K Q J 10 8 7
              ♣ A Q 8 2
```

S	W	N	E
	Miss E.		Miss A.
The	Clutter-	Bro.	Clutter-
Abbot	buck	Paulo	buck
	2 ♠	2 NT	No
4 ◇	No	4 ♡	No
6 ◇	End		

The Misses Clutterbuck were so heavily made up it was difficult to assess their age. At a charitable guess they might have been in their late seventies. The monastery team had been surprised to discover

that they favoured the Blue Club system with a mini-no-trump throughout.

Miss Clutterbuck (West) opened with a weak two-bid, and when the Abbot propelled himself into a small slam in diamonds she led the king of spades (modified Roman leads, according to her scorecard). The Abbot leaned forward anxiously to see what cards awaited him and Brother Paulo revealed a treasure-laden dummy. There were four precious stones embedded in it – the missing club honour, the ace of trumps and two good heart pictures.

The Abbot ruffed the king of spades and played off the king and queen of trumps. This provided the unwelcome news that West had the outstanding trump. If East had started with three trumps a simple avoidance play in clubs would have seen declarer home. He would have cashed the king of clubs and led twice towards his own club holding, ensuring three club tricks and either a club ruff or, if East ruffed in front of him, a heart ruff after a heart had been discarded on the fourth club.

The Abbot pulled his thoughts together. It was pleasant enough day-dreaming about how he could have impressed everyone on some other distribution, but what could he do now? Still undecided, he drew the last trump and played the ace and king of clubs, obtaining a complete count on the hand. East guarded the clubs and West the spades, so the conditions were present for a straightforward double squeeze. Unfortunately, however, he could see no way to rectify the count without destroying one of his menaces.

The Abbot drummed his long fingers on the table. This mannerism seemed to aggravate Miss Clutterbuck (East), who was pointedly sucking in air between her teeth. The Abbot stopped for a time and then started up again.

"Grieg's Piano Sonata in A flat, if I'm not mistaken," remarked Miss Clutterbuck (West) to her partner. "An excessively lengthy piece at the best of times."

The Abbot considered the chances of a throw-in. The snag about this was that he could not be sure which opponent held the queen of hearts. Suddenly it struck him that he could rectify the count by leading a spade from dummy and discarding a heart. The knave of hearts was not essential to his plan.

Miss Clutterbuck (West) won the spade trick and switched to a heart, but the hand was over. When the Abbot cashed the last trump, this was the end position:

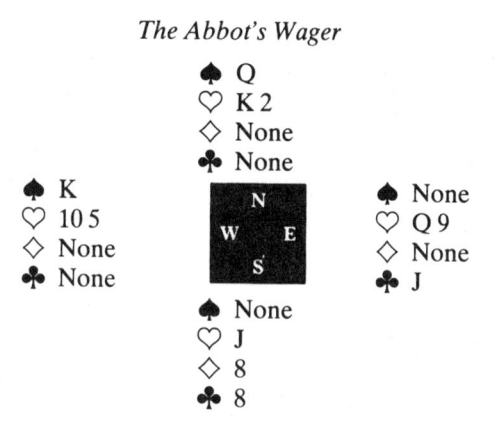

```
                    ♠ Q
                    ♡ K 2
                    ◇ None
                    ♣ None
   ♠ K              ┌─────────┐       ♠ None
   ♡ 10 5           │    N    │       ♡ Q 9
   ◇ None           │  W   E  │       ◇ None
   ♣ None           │    S    │       ♣ J
                    └─────────┘
                    ♠ None
                    ♡ J
                    ◇ 8
                    ♣ 8
```

Neither defender could hold the hearts and the dummy's two of hearts took the twelfth trick.

"How many IMPs do you think we gained on that lot?" said the Abbot to Brother Paulo as they waited in the corridor for the other room to finish play.

"Well, not much in it, I think."

"Not much in it? What on earth are you talking about? Surely we should get a slam swing on that last hand I played?"

"Well, er . . . it is possible, but you see . . ."

"Apart from the fact that we only had a 29-count, I can scarcely imagine they'll play the hand the way I did. I'll tell you what I'll do. I'll bet you a dozen bottles of Brother Michael's best sherry that we gain a slam swing on the board."

"At San Giovanni in Italia we never were being allowed to make bettings."

"I'll arrange a dispensation for you," said the Abbot. "Ah, they've finished!"

The Abbot strode into the other room and eased his capacious frame into one of the red armchairs.

"I found a way home in six diamonds on board 24," he announced proudly, "and I've had a small bet with our friend here that it'll be a slam swing."

"Well done, Abbot. You win the bet easily," said Brother Lucius with a wry smile. "They bid *seven* diamonds against us."

"Oh, that's bad luck, Brother Paulo," said the Abbot, trying not to look pleased. "I had no intention of winning the bet in this manner, but it makes little difference. They would doubtless have gone down in six also."

"Somewhat unlikely, seeing that they made seven," commented Brother Lucius drily. "Declarer ruffed four rounds of spades in hand, then squeezed me with dummy's last trump. A simple dummy reversal. This was the ending:"

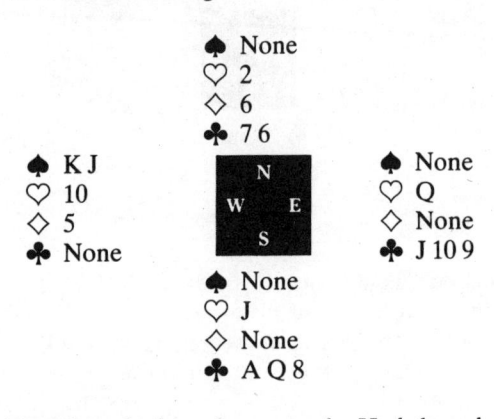

```
              ♠ None
              ♡ 2
              ◇ 6
              ♣ 7 6
  ♠ K J                      ♠ None
  ♡ 10        N              ♡ Q
  ◇ 5      W     E           ◇ None
  ♣ None       S             ♣ J 10 9
              ♠ None
              ♡ J
              ◇ None
              ♣ A Q 8
```

The Abbot thought for a few seconds. Had there been enough entries to the table for all this?

"You didn't tell me the opening lead," he said, turning suspiciously towards Brother Xavier. "You were on lead, weren't you? What was your lead?"

"Er ... the ace of spades, I believe," gulped Brother Xavier nervously.

"Well, well. I never thought the day would dawn when a teammate of mine would make such a lead," observed the Abbot with a sorrowful smile. "On the lead of a trump, automatic against a grand slam, declarer would have no chance. Your ace of spades was hardly likely to stand up, was it?"

"Well, I don't know, Abbot," retaliated Brother Xavier bravely. "Only last Tuesday at the £1 table you bid that grand slam in spades, and I led the ..."

"Yes, yes," interrupted the Abbot testily. "Well, I make it we have won the match by 6 IMPs anyway, so let's just forget this unfortunate affair."

"I will not be so soon forgetting, Abbot," said Brother Paulo. "It takes a quite long time to sip down twelve bottles of sherry!"

The LeStrange Chalice

For nigh on forty years the second Saturday after Michaelmas had seen the two principal orders of the community clash in a special challenge match for the LeStrange Chalice. This superb example of early Georgian silver had been donated to the monastery by the family of the Abbot LeStrange and seemed to inspire the monks to perform to the very limits of their various abilities.

The Mendacians, a cunning and devious Order captained by their star player, Brother Lucius, usually started as favourites; but the Archimedeans, a mathematical Order captained by the Abbot, had won the trophy the previous year and were quietly hopeful of retaining it. One of the longest suits ever dealt at the monastery appeared on Board 23.

Game all, dealer South

```
                    ♠ K 9 5 3
                    ♡ K J
                    ◇ Q 10 5
                    ♣ K 9 6 4
     ♠ 8 7 6 2           N           ♠ A Q J 10 4
     ♡ 8                             ♡ None
     ◇ 8 7 4 2      W       E        ◇ K J 9 3
     ♣ 10 8 7 3         S            ♣ A Q J 5
                    ♠ None
                    ♡ A Q 10 9 7 6 5 4 3 2
                    ◇ A 6
                    ♣ 2
```

Room 1:	S	W	N	E
	Bro.	Bro.	Bro.	Bro.
	Xavier	Michael	Sextus	Tacitus
	No	No	1 NT	dble
	6 ♡	End		

Brother Xavier passed in a bored tone on the South cards, a typical Mendacian manoeuvre. When his partner opened a weak

no-trump and East doubled, however, he could not resist a spectacular leap to six hearts.

"Did you say *six* hearts?" gasped his partner, beginning to regret his dubious opening bid.

When the bidding ran round to East, Brother Tacitus refrained from doubling. No one had forced South to bid six hearts, so he obviously had some wild freak.

Declarer ruffed the spade lead, drew the outstanding trump and led a club, intending to insert the nine and endplay East, whose double marked him with most of the missing high cards. However, Brother Michael, the monastery wine steward sitting West, defended well by inserting the club ten. Dummy had to cover and when East took the ace and played back the queen of clubs declarer was left without resource.

At the next table the same contract was reached in more orthodox fashion:

Game all, dealer South

```
                 ♠ K 9 5 3
                 ♡ K J
                 ◇ Q 10 5
                 ♣ K 9 6 4
  ♠ 8 7 6 2                      ♠ A Q J 10 4
  ♡ 8              N             ♡ None
  ◇ 8 7 4 2    W       E         ◇ K J 9 3
  ♣ 10 8 7 3       S             ♣ A Q J 5
                 ♠ None
                 ♡ A Q 10 9 7 6 5 4 3 2
                 ◇ A 6
                 ♣ 2
```

Room 2:	S	W	N	E
	Bro.	Bro.	Bro.	Bro.
	Damien	James	Dunstan	Paulo
	2 ♡	No	3 NT	4 ♡ (!)
	6 ♡	End		

Once again the eight of spades was led and ruffed in hand by

young Brother Damien, who saw at once that if East held both the king of diamonds and the ace of clubs, he could be thrown in at trick 11.

The position soon became equally clear to Brother Paulo in the East seat. In an attempt to confuse the declarer he kept $\diamond$ K alone and ♣ A J as his last three cards. However, Brother Damien was not deceived. The bid of four hearts by his opponent strongly suggested 5–0–4–4 distribution rather than 5–0–5–3. The ace of diamonds brought down the king and the queen of diamonds provided the twelfth trick.

Room 3.

At the next table Brother Aelred held the South cards. In his view the long suit clearly demanded a pre-emptive opening.

"Is it my bid?" he asked nervously. "Well, er . . . six hearts."

Deciding that if he defeated the contract he would obtain a good score anyway, Brother Zac passed in the East seat. The eight of spades was led and covered by the nine and ten.

Brother Aelred's eyes were aglow. He could actually see a chance of bringing his bold bid home. Surely all he needed was to find West with the ace of clubs. Unfortunately East had paused for a moment or two before passing out the slam, so it was a good bet that he held both the missing aces. Brother Aelred decided to try for a squeeze instead. It was quite easy, he had read a rather intriguing book about it in the monastery library. All you had to do, apparently, was to give up a trick and play off all your trumps. Deciding to give this new technique a try, he threw his singleton club away on the first trick instead of ruffing.

Brother Zac, who did not view this development with much relish, returned the queen of clubs as smoothly as he could, but Brother Aelred just looked at him in amazement, discarded his losing diamond and claimed the contract.

"You could have made it much more difficult for me," he informed Brother Zac sternly.

"I don't see how," came the reply.

"Well, if you return a trump I'd have to play for a squeeze," continued Brother Aelred learnedly.

"Of course," said Brother Zac. "Silly of me. Sorry, partner."

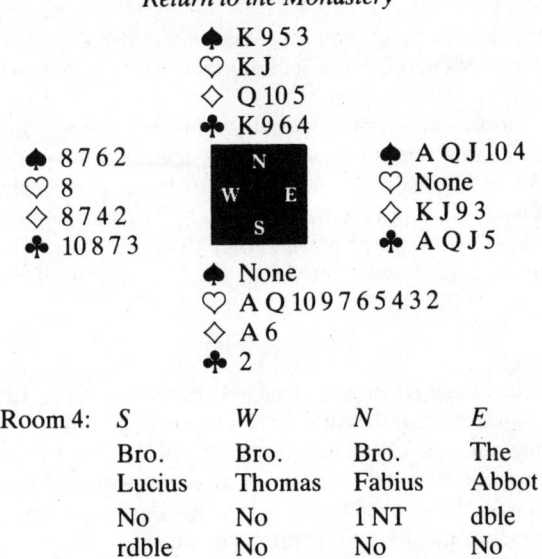

```
                ♠ K 9 5 3
                ♡ K J
                ♢ Q 10 5
                ♣ K 9 6 4
♠ 8 7 6 2                        ♠ A Q J 10 4
♡ 8              N              ♡ None
♢ 8 7 4 2     W     E           ♢ K J 9 3
♣ 10 8 7 3        S             ♣ A Q J 5
                ♠ None
                ♡ A Q 10 9 7 6 5 4 3 2
                ♢ A 6
                ♣ 2
```

Room 4:	S	W	N	E
	Bro.	Bro.	Bro.	The
	Lucius	Thomas	Fabius	Abbot
	No	No	1 NT	dble
	rdble	No	No	No

Brother Lucius also rated the South hand a stand-out pass by Mendacian methods. When his partner opened one no-trump and the Abbot doubled, he redoubled in the tone of a man going to his own funeral.

This call ran round to the Abbot, who glared at Brother Lucius suspiciously. Was this another of his notorious five-point redoubles? Refusing to be intimidated, the Abbot passed and slapped the queen of spades on the table.

"I hope I haven't let you down, partner," said Brother Lucius, laying down his dummy. "I couldn't open with only 10 points, but my hand may be useful to you."

Everyone gasped at the sight of the heart suit, so long that it stretched right across the table.

"Yes, I see what you mean," replied Brother Fabius, gathering in the first trick. "Well, unless I'm really lucky and the king of diamonds is singleton, I'm going to have to give you the last trick, Abbot."

The clock of the monastery chapel could be heard sounding eleven o'clock as the players gathered expectantly round their team captains to announce their scores. They soon reached the fateful board.

"Board 23?" asked the Abbot apprehensively. "The two North–South scores first, please."

"Plus 1430," replied Brother Damien happily.

"Same again," added Brother Aelred proudly.

"And on the East–West cards?" enquired the Abbot.

"Plus 100," declared Brother Michael.

"Board 24?" continued the Abbot hopefully.

"Just a minute," interrupted Brother Michael. "What happened to you on Board 23, Abbot?"

"Oh, er . . . nothing interesting. The slam was not bid, in fact the hand was passed out at the one-level."

"At the one-level? Who by? What was the result?"

"It was played by North," said the Abbot, "for a score of hrff . . . hrff . . . minus hrff . . . hrff . . . hundred and ten."

"Sorry, did you say 110 or 210, Abbot?" asked Brother Aelred politely. "I'm writing all the scores down on my card."

"I wish you'd listen more carefully," replied the Abbot in a gruff tone. "As I said, we lost 2710. Our friend Brother Thomas allowed himself to be bamboozled by one of Lucius's manoeuvres. I wanted to spare his feelings. Next board?"

The Abbot's Invitation

"Are you doing anything tomorrow evening, Brother Aelred?" asked the Abbot pleasantly, as they met one morning in the cloisters.

Brother Aelred pricked up his ears. What an honour! No one from the 5p table had ever been asked to play in the Abbot's private Tuesday night game before. Perhaps the Abbot had heard about that tricky 3 NT he had made the other day.

"No, Abbot," he replied innocently. "Why do you ask?"

"The Amaryllis Recorder Quartet, one of the most distinguished groups in our Order, are giving a recital of fifteenth-century monastic psalm settings in the refectory. I myself will unfortunately be engaged in other duties but I thought you might like to attend."

Before Brother Aelred could recover his breath, the Abbot strode into the monastery cardroom and took a seat at the £1 table.

Love all, dealer South

```
              ♠ 10 7 3
              ♡ 9 6 5
              ◇ K Q 10 3
              ♣ 8 3 2
♠ Q J 9 6 4            ♠ 8
♡ Q 7          N       ♡ J 10 4 2
◇ J 7 4 2    W   E     ◇ 9 6
♣ J 4          S       ♣ A K 9 7 6 5
              ♠ A K 5 2
              ♡ A K 8 3
              ◇ A 8 5
              ♣ Q 10
```

S	W	N	E
Bro.	The	Bro.	Bro.
Lucius	Abbot	Paulo	Xavier
2 NT	No	3 NT	End

The Abbot led the queen of spades which held the trick, Brother Lucius contributing the two from hand. The Abbot paused briefly to reflect on the likely lie of the spade suit. His partner would clearly have unblocked from A 8 doubleton but he might have started with

K 8 doubleton. It was also possible that the eight was an encouraging card from king to three. Of course if declarer had four spades he would obviously have guaranteed three tricks in the suit by winning immediately, or at the very least played the five from hand to encourage a continuation. That possibility could definitely be ruled out.

Satisfied with his analysis, the Abbot continued with the six of spades. To his amazement the dummy's ten won and East signalled with the seven of clubs. Now Brother Lucius needed only to bring in the diamond suit. Entering his hand with a heart, he led a small diamond towards the table. The Abbot, still thinking about the spades, dropped the four. When the king won and declarer returned to the ace, the Abbot made an attempt to disguise his mistake by following with the seven. On the next trick, perforce, he produced the two.

The Abbot's discomfort was evident to Brother Lucius. "The Abbot has played a clever game here," he said to his partner. "Well, I dare say I'll look foolish, but I'm going to put in the ten. Aha," he continued when the ten won, "you played a clever game there, Abbot, you nearly fooled me."

It was some time before the Abbot had a chance to gain his revenge.

Game all, dealer South

```
              ♠ K J 6 4
              ♡ J 7
              ♢ A J 10 7 4 3
              ♣ 7
♠ 9 7 3                        ♠ A 10 8 2
♡ A K 5          N             ♡ 4 3
♢ 8          W       E         ♢ 9 6 5 2
♣ K Q 10 8 4 3   S             ♣ J 9 6
              ♠ Q 5
              ♡ Q 10 9 8 6 2
              ♢ K Q
              ♣ A 5 2
```

S	W	N	E
The	Bro.	Bro.	Bro.
Abbot	Lucius	Xavier	Paulo
1 ♡	2 ♣	2 ♢	No
2 ♡	No	3 ♡	No
4 ♡	End		

[135]

Brother Lucius led the king of hearts and switched to the king of clubs, the only defence to trouble declarer. The Abbot assessed his prospects as distinctly grim. The only genuine chance appeared to be that West held a doubleton diamond and A K of hearts alone. The Abbot was loath to entrust a vulnerable game to such a slender lifeline; perhaps he could improve on it. West had indicated twelve or thirteen points already, so it was a fair bet that East held the spade ace. Yes, of course, here at last was the chance he had been waiting for!

The Abbot played dummy's small club and followed with the five from hand. Silence reigned as Brother Lucius digested the implications of this development. Eventually he pulled another round of trumps with his ace. The Abbot could feel his heart pounding. Would Lucius fall for the trap? It was obvious from his lengthy deliberation that he didn't hold the spade ace, anyway.

Brother Lucius played a card and the Abbot steeled himself to glance down and see what it was. The card that met his eyes possessed a quiet beauty he had never appreciated before: it was the club queen.

"Drawing trumps and the rest are mine," said the Abbot jubilantly, facing his hand with a flourish. "I need hardly add that if you've got all the diamonds, Brother Paulo, together with the ace of spades, the last trump will squeeze you."

Brother Lucius frowned at his remaining cards. Should he have read the situation? Had he missed a clue somewhere? Brother Paulo supplied it.

"If I am holding the ace of clubs, partner," said the Italian, "am I not overtaking and returning a heart?"

"Perhaps you am, I mean are," said Brother Lucius irritably. "I make the rubber 1470."

1470? That number rang a bell, thought the Abbot. Ah yes, the date of St. Lubrigand's moving quartet for recorders, "De Mortibus Sanctorum".

"That reminds me, Lucius," he said. "Are you doing anything tomorrow night?"

The Chancellor's Cup

The Abbot set great store on achieving a good result in the Chancellor's Cup, the national inter-monastery championship. Any promising youngsters thinking of a monastic career were much more likely to be attracted to a monastery with a successful first team.

This year the two ante-post favourites, the Monastery of St. Titus and the Sutton Scotney Friary, were well clear of their rivals in the round-robin and therefore met in a 40-board final on the Sunday.

Game all, dealer South

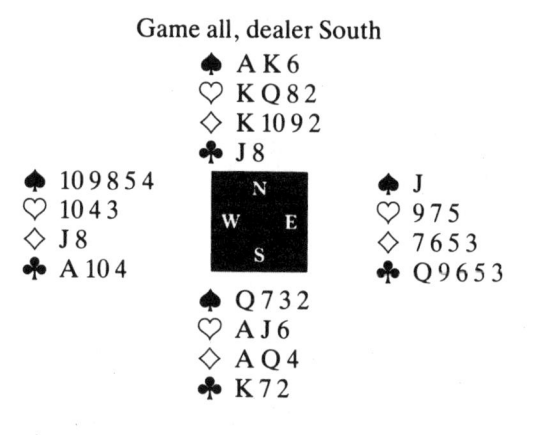

♠ A K 6
♡ K Q 8 2
◇ K 10 9 2
♣ J 8

♠ 10 9 8 5 4
♡ 10 4 3
◇ J 8
♣ A 10 4

♠ J
♡ 9 7 5
◇ 7 6 5 3
♣ Q 9 6 5 3

♠ Q 7 3 2
♡ A J 6
◇ A Q 4
♣ K 7 2

On Board 7 Brother Lucius opened a 16–18 no-trump on the South cards and replied two spades to the Abbot's Stayman enquiry. The Abbot paused, fingering an earlobe thoughtfully and gazing out of a nearby window where it had just started to rain. A limit bid of 4 NT would describe his values well, but would Brother Lucius take the bid as Blackwood?

"Four no-trumps," said the Abbot eventually, reflecting that if this led to the wrong contract he would be well placed to blame his partner.

Now it was Brother Lucius who paused. Was this a limit bid or did the Abbot intend it as Blackwood? Even with his rock-bottom minimum, he thought, it must be safer to bid on. If they ended in a thin slam, at least he would be playing it.

Over Lucius's five heart response the Abbot bid an abrupt 6 NT, hoping for the best. This had been the somewhat undistinguished auction:

S	W	N	E
Bro.	Friar	The	Friar
Lucius	Tuffill	Abbot	Rowe
1 NT	No	2 ♣	No
2 ♠	No	4 NT	No
5 ♡	No	6 NT	End

Friar Tuffill, a powerful man with enormous forearms protruding from his cassock, led the ten of spades, and Brother Lucius won in dummy, noting the fall of the knave from East. The spade situation seemed rather unpromising, thought Brother Lucius. It looked as if he would have to pick up four tricks in diamonds and find East with the ace of clubs.

The ace and queen of diamonds produced the knave, and Brother Lucius continued with a spade towards the dummy's K 6, West electing to split his equals. When the last red card was cashed, this was the ending:

```
                    ♠ 6
                    ♡ Q
                    ◇ None
                    ♣ J 8
    ♠ 9 5          ┌─────────┐      ♠ None
    ♡ None         │    N    │      ♡ None
    ◇ None         │ W     E │      ◇ None
    ♣ A 10         │    S    │      ♣ Q 9 6 5
                   └─────────┘
                    ♠ Q 7
                    ♡ None
                    ◇ None
                    ♣ K 7
```

On the queen of hearts all three players threw a club, and declarer continued with a club to the bare king, secure in the knowledge that whether West's last club was the ace or queen the slam was home.

"That was a trifle fortunate," observed the Abbot. "You realised you could have passed four no-trumps?"

"Of course," Brother Lucius replied. "I nearly did."

St. Titus was in the lead but the match was still open when the following hand appeared late in the second half:

N–S game, dealer West

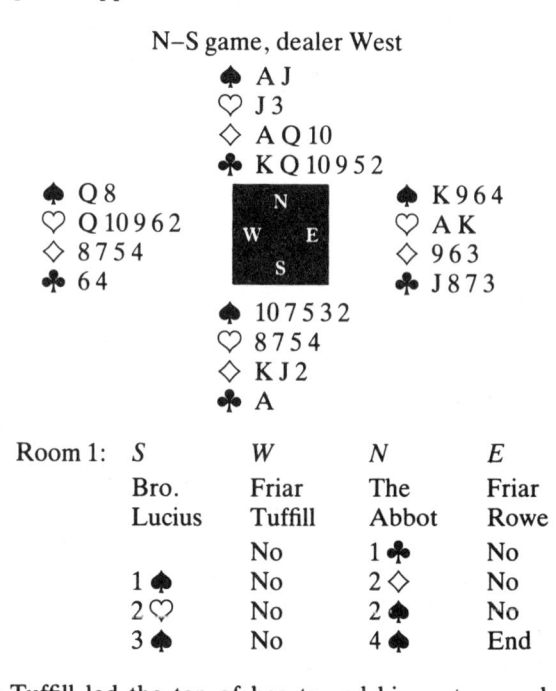

♠ A J
♡ J 3
◇ A Q 10
♣ K Q 10 9 5 2

♠ Q 8
♡ Q 10 9 6 2
◇ 8 7 5 4
♣ 6 4

♠ K 9 6 4
♡ A K
◇ 9 6 3
♣ J 8 7 3

♠ 10 7 5 3 2
♡ 8 7 5 4
◇ K J 2
♣ A

Room 1:	S	W	N	E
	Bro.	Friar	The	Friar
	Lucius	Tuffill	Abbot	Rowe
		No	1 ♣	No
	1 ♠	No	2 ◇	No
	2 ♡	No	2 ♠	No
	3 ♠	No	4 ♠	End

Friar Tuffill led the ten of hearts and his partner cashed two rounds before returning a club. Brother Lucius captured in hand, thankful to have escaped a third round of hearts. Even so, prospects were bleak. If West held a doubleton honour in trumps, including the 8 or 9, then a trump coup might be engineered. This was surely the best chance.

Brother Lucius played a spade to the 8, knave and king and won the diamond return on the table. After cashing the ace of spades and the king-queen of clubs, on which he threw his two heart losers, he ruffed a club and cashed two more diamonds.

"620?" said Brother Lucius to East, showing him his 10 7 of trumps.

"I somehow don't think we're destined to win this match, partner," remarked East with a smile, replacing his cards in the wallet. "I doubt whether our lads will find this contract."

Room 2:	S	W	N	E
	Friar		Friar	
	Long-	Bro.	Catch-	Bro.
	Fox	Xavier	pole	Paulo
		No	1 ♣	No
	1 ♠	No	3 ♣	No
	3 NT	End		

Brother Paulo, sitting East, won the ten of hearts lead and cashed his other heart honour. Since South was surely marked with the ace of clubs, Brother Paulo attempted a form of Deschapelles Coup, leading the king of spades.

Friar Long-Fox inspected this card for several moments. Apparently the hearts were blocked, so even if East held a club stop the contract might still succeed. It seemed dangerous to duck, because the defence might make two hearts, two spades and a club.

"Ace, please," directed the friar, "and a small club."

East was soon in with the knave of clubs and the defenders cashed four more tricks to put the contract three down vulnerable.

"Was the queen of spades doubleton?" enquired Friar Long-Fox.

"Yes, I'm afraid so," replied Brother Xavier.

"Splendid!" exclaimed the friar. "What a fine hand to show our brethren back at the friary!"

Most of the less successful monasteries had stayed on for a Swiss Teams event on the Sunday, so there was a large and varied gathering of monks in attendance as the local mayor presented the prizes.

"I must congratulate you, Abbot, on an exceptionally high standard of play over the weekend," said the Mayor, as he handed over the ornate silver cup. "A round of applause, everyone, for the Monastery of St. Titus!"

"That's most kind of you," replied the Abbot, pausing to direct a triumphant smile into the lens of the *Monastery News* photographer. "What has pleased me most has not been our victory but the fine sporting spirit in which the event has been played. I must also pay tribute to the excellent bidding and cardplay of our opponents in the final: the worthy friars of er . . . that well-known establishment . . ."

"The Sutton Scotney Friary," prompted the Mayor.

". . . the Sutton Scotney Friary," concluded the Abbot gratefully.

[140]

After the presentation the monastery team made good speed towards the bar. "And now a small celebration. Whatever our own tendencies may be," the Abbot looked sharply at Brother Paulo, "we must respect the principles of others. Barman, a round of your best lemonade!"

When the Bell Tolls

As Brother Aelred heaved on the bellrope that heralded the four o'clock Matins, the deep sound of the old bell had a hypnotic effect, and his thoughts drifted back to the previous evening's rubber game.

He remembered particularly well the following hand, where he had held the South cards.

Love all, dealer South

```
              ♠ 10 6 5
              ♡ A K Q
              ◇ A 9 6
              ♣ Q 10 9 7
   ♠ 7 3                      ♠ K 4
   ♡ J 9 7 5 3      N         ♡ 10 8 2
   ◇ 10 8 7 5 2   W   E       ◇ K Q J 4
   ♣ 2              S         ♣ K J 6 3
              ♠ A Q J 9 8 2
              ♡ 6 4
              ◇ 3
              ♣ A 8 5 4
```

S	W	N	E
Bro.	Bishop	The	Bro.
Aelred	Benton	Abbot	Lucius
1 ♠	No	2 ♣	No
3 ♠	No	6 ♠	End

West, an Anglican clergyman visiting the monastery to attend a course on trump reduction, led the two of clubs; and while declarer surveyed the dummy Brother Lucius did some quick calculation. Surely the lead was a singleton, and with the king of trumps well placed declarer would have the easiest of rides to twelve tricks.

Steeped as he was in the long traditions of the Mendacian Order of monks, Brother Lucius soon constructed an obstacle to put in declarer's path. When declarer reached for dummy's seven of clubs, Brother Lucius followed smoothly with the king.

Winning with the ace, Brother Aelred smiled confidently to himself. The king of clubs was almost certainly a singleton, and there was therefore no need to take the spade finesse. Indeed it could be fatal to do so, since a losing finesse would surely be followed by a club ruff. Delighted at having this chance to impress the Abbot, he played off the ace and queen of trumps and subsequently went one off.

"Did you miss my sermon on elimination play last week, Brother Aelred?" demanded the Abbot with what he believed was a friendly smile. "If you take the precaution of removing the red suits before playing the second trump, Brother Lucius's false card will fall on stony ground. He will either have to give a ruff-and-discard or return a club into dummy's queen-ten."

Brother Aelred stared resentfully at Brother Lucius, who was modestly studying the cardroom ceiling. Why couldn't he just play bridge normally, thought Brother Aelred, like everyone else?

The tolling of the bell lost some of its urgency as Brother Aelred's arms began to tire. He closed his eyes and tried to recall another interesting slam that had fallen his way the night before.

Game all, dealer South

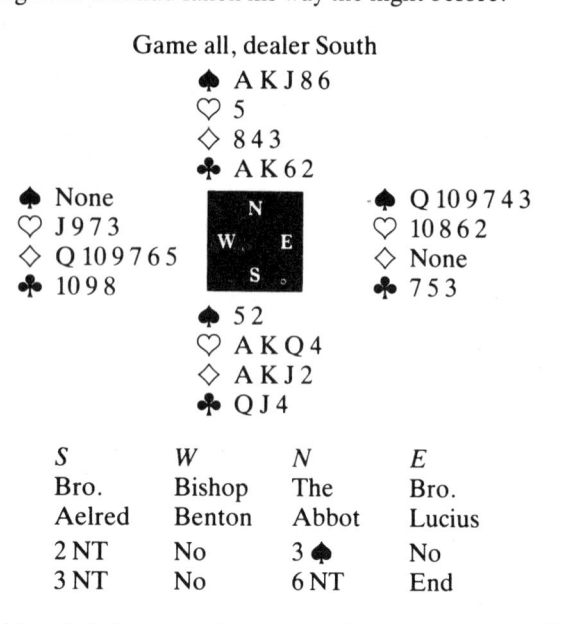

```
                  ♠ A K J 8 6
                  ♡ 5
                  ◇ 8 4 3
                  ♣ A K 6 2
  ♠ None                          ♠ Q 10 9 7 4 3
  ♡ J 9 7 3            N          ♡ 10 8 6 2
  ◇ Q 10 9 7 6 5   W     E        ◇ None
  ♣ 10 9 8            S           ♣ 7 5 3
                  ♠ 5 2
                  ♡ A K Q 4
                  ◇ A K J 2
                  ♣ Q J 4
```

S	W	N	E
Bro.	Bishop	The	Bro.
Aelred	Benton	Abbot	Lucius
2 NT	No	3 ♠	No
3 NT	No	6 NT	End

The Bishop led the ten of clubs and declarer won in hand. When a

spade to the king and a diamond to the ace revealed the unfortunate lie of those suits, Brother Aelred marked time by cashing the club suit. He then started on the hearts, and each defender in turn could see a throw-in looming up. The indignity of being endplayed by so lowly a player as Brother Aelred was clearly not to be contemplated, so they both began to toss away their high hearts with the determination of sailors bailing out a sinking lifeboat.

When Brother Aelred finally played the four of hearts, he was staggered to find that it gathered the three and the two, and the trick was his.

"Nicely played, Brother Aelred!" exclaimed the Abbot, entering the unexpected windfall on his scorepad. "That was rather an awkward hand for a player such as yourself."

"It was nothing, Abbot," Brother Aelred replied in a careless tone. "I was looking at this type of hand only yesterday. Our distinguished guest had to guard the diamonds, Brother Lucius had to guard the spades, so no one could hold the hearts. Quite a common type of squeeze."

As he emerged from his pleasant reminiscences, Brother Aelred glanced down at his watch. 3.59 a.m.! He flew down the belfry staircase, entered the organ loft and seated himself on the hard wooden bench. As he struck up the opening chords of Stainer's "Magnificat", no sound came at all.

Walking round the back of the organ, he saw Brother Rupert gazing vacantly out of a window.

"Wake up, Brother Rupert! Start pumping, please! We can't afford to spend our time just day-dreaming, can we?"

Anyone for Tennis?

"May I speak to you, Abbot?" said Brother Lucius, as they left the chapel after Vespers.

"Very well, but be brief. I have a novitiates' bidding class in five minutes."

"I received a missive this morning from my cousin, Sister Grace, challenging us to a 32-boarder. The proposed stake is £2 an IMP, to be paid by the losers to a charity of the winners' choosing."

"Hmm. A surprisingly bold suggestion on their part," replied the Abbot. "Write back immediately accepting the offer before they think better of it. We should raise quite a tidy sum for the new tennis court."

"And what about a venue, Abbot? I understand the convent has an even stricter rule about visitors than we have here at St. Titus."

"Better make it the Turk's Head at Bursledon," advised the Abbot. "Their roast-beef sandwiches are sustaining. We can order a couple of rounds each for half-time."

One sunny evening a week or so later the Abbot's heavily-laden Austin Seven pulled into the Turk's Head carpark, just as nine or ten nuns were parking their bicycles in the far corner. Obviously they were taking the match seriously and had brought some supporters with them.

"Evening, Sister Grace," said the Abbot, as he levered himself out of the car. "Is the Mother Superior with you?"

"No. Not yet, Abbot. But she did say she would come along later to watch the last few boards. Shall we go in?"

E–W game, dealer West

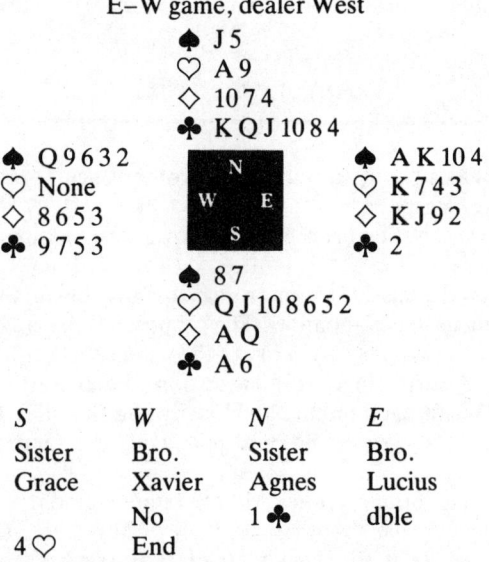

```
                    ♠ J 5
                    ♡ A 9
                    ♢ 10 7 4
                    ♣ K Q J 10 8 4
♠ Q 9 6 3 2                          ♠ A K 10 4
♡ None                               ♡ K 7 4 3
♢ 8 6 5 3                            ♢ K J 9 2
♣ 9 7 5 3                            ♣ 2
                    ♠ 8 7
                    ♡ Q J 10 8 6 5 2
                    ♢ A Q
                    ♣ A 6
```

S	W	N	E
Sister	Bro.	Sister	Bro.
Grace	Xavier	Agnes	Lucius
	No	1 ♣	dble
4 ♡	End		

The three of spades was led to the five, king and seven, and Brother Lucius returned his singleton club. His intention was clear. When he won the trump king he would put his partner in for a club ruff.

Sister Grace was also aware of this unsavoury possibility. Spotting a counter, she ran the club return to dummy's king and led a diamond to the queen, which held. Her plan now was to cash the ace of diamonds, cross to the ace of trumps and throw her last spade on the ten of diamonds. If East held the knave of diamonds as well as the king, he would have to take the trick and the spade link would be broken.

Brother Lucius realised declarer's intentions and put up a typically imaginative defence. On the ace of diamonds he threw his king, and two tricks later he underplayed dummy's ten of diamonds with the nine.

Sister Grace adjusted her spectacles suspiciously. It certainly seemed as if East had started with ♠ A K x x x ♡ K x x x ♢ K 9 x ♣ x, and had ditched the diamond king to avoid having to win the third round. In that case the contract would be impossible. She was therefore forced to assume that East had concealed either the spade

queen or the diamond knave. Since the first of these plays would have been unusually far-sighted and the second well within the devious capabilities of Brother Lucius, Sister Grace eventually ran the diamond, throwing her spade, and ended up with an unexpected overtrick.

"Still up to your old tricks, cousin?" she remarked sharply.

Out of curiosity Sister Agnes picked up West's cards from the table. "Sister Myrtle will sacrifice in four spades on these cards," she pointed out helpfully. "On a club lead doesn't declarer come to seven tricks in trumps, two diamonds and the king of hearts, as the cards lie?"

"I don't expect they'll bid it," replied Brother Xavier, looking worried. "I only had a two-count and it was vulnerable against not."

"You don't know Sister Myrtle," said Sister Agnes. "And South will double. I'm afraid you must resign yourselves to a double game swing."

Meanwhile in the other room the Abbot and Brother Paulo were experiencing a rough ride on another deal.

N–S game, dealer West

```
              ♠ A 5 2
              ♡ 10
              ◇ J 8 6 5
              ♣ A K 8 3 2
♠ K J 8                        ♠ None
♡ A 8 5          N             ♡ K Q J 6 4 2
◇ A 10 7 3 2   W   E           ◇ K Q 9 4
♣ J 9            S             ♣ Q 6 4
              ♠ Q 10 9 7 6 4 3
              ♡ 9 7 3
              ◇ None
              ♣ 10 7 5
```

S	W	N	E
Sister	The	Sister	Bro.
Myrtle	Abbot	Edith	Paulo
	1 NT	No	4 ♡
4 ♠	dble	End	

The Abbot led the ace of hearts and raised his eyebrows as the magnificent dummy was laid out. He continued with a small heart,

[147]

hoping to make both his trump honours if the dummy could be forced again later.

"Ruff low," requested Sister Myrtle in a business-like voice. "Diamond."

Crossing backwards and forwards, Sister Myrtle ruffed all four diamonds, arriving at this position:

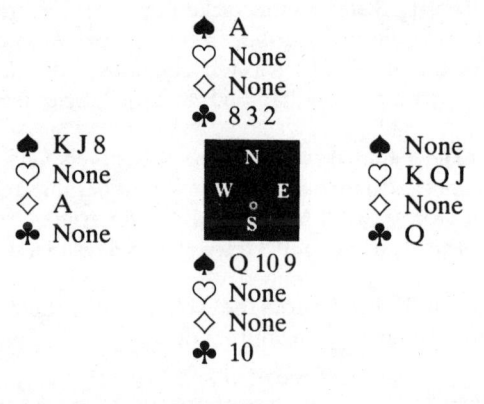

Sister Myrtle now exited to East's club queen, and the heart return killed one of the Abbot's hoped-for trump tricks.

"Prettily played, partner," said Sister Edith. "I ought to have redoubled, but sometimes you do take a slight risk and . . ."

"Not at this vulnerability, partner," interrupted Sister Myrtle. "I had an eight-card suit, after all."

"Or was it nine?" asked Brother Paulo mournfully.

The monastery team had barely finished comparing scores when the door opened and in flowed the serene figure of the Mother Superior, followed by the four members of the convent team.

"A good evening to you, Abbot," she said in a quiet voice. "Sister Grace tells me that you all played splendidly and the final margin was just 46 IMPs to our team."

The Abbot rose to his feet, looking somewhat embarrassed.

"I understand that our St. Clare Mission will benefit by some £92," continued the Mother Superior. "It really is most kind of you. I must thank you all for making such a generous contribution."

Brother Rupert's Comeback

Brother Lucius gave his hand a cursory glance, then folded his cards and placed three amber rosary beads in the middle of the table.

"Your 50p," he said, "and up £1."

"I'm out," declared Brother Aelred, throwing his cards in.

"Jumping Jehosophat!" exclaimed Brother Xavier. "Our Superior has arrived. I thought you said he was out for the afternoon."

"Right. Don't panic," said Brother Lucius, cool as ever. "Just deal the cards again and pretend we're playing bridge."

"But I haven't played bridge for years," complained Brother Rupert. "I'll never manage it."

"Pull yourself together," came the stern reply. "If the Abbot finds out we've been playing poker again, it'll be a week on St. Stephen's Penance at the very least."

Love all, dealer West

```
                    ♠ 9
                    ♡ A J 9 8 6 5 4 3 2
                    ◇ K 8 3
                    ♣ None
    ♠ 7 6 2                           ♠ 8 5 4 3
    ♡ 7            N                  ♡ K Q
    ◇ A J 10 9 7 6 5  W    E          ◇ Q 4 2
    ♣ 7 2             S               ♣ Q 9 4 3
                    ♠ A K Q J 10
                    ♡ 10
                    ◇ None
                    ♣ A K J 10 8 6 5
```

S	W	N	E
Bro.	Bro.	Bro.	Bro.
Rupert	Aelred	Xavier	Lucius
	3 ◇	4 ♡	5 ◇
6 ♣	6 ◇	dble	No
6 ♠	End		

As Brother Rupert finished sorting his cards, the Abbot arrived

at the table and peered nosily over his shoulder. What bad luck to pick up such an exceptional hand, thought Brother Rupert.

Realising that Brother Rupert would have little chance of negotiating a full auction convincingly, the other three monks co-operated well by jamming the auction up to five diamonds before he had an opportunity to bid. But Brother Rupert was not embarrassed. "Six clubs," he said firmly. Brother Aelred, who always tended to bid his values at least twice, competed with six diamonds on the West cards. North doubled loudly, but Brother Rupert pressed on to six spades. Brother Xavier passed with a sigh.

The ace of diamonds was led and Brother Rupert ruffed in hand. He now played the knave of clubs, hoping to limit his losses to one club trick. Interesting, thought the Abbot; if West covers with the queen, declarer must refuse to ruff in the dummy.

When West produced the seven, declarer threw a heart from the table and Brother Lucius, reluctant to release his control on declarer's side suit, played the three.

Pursuing his original plan, Brother Rupert continued with a small club and threw another heart from table. Brother Lucius won the trick and fired back a third club, which was ruffed by West and overruffed in the dummy. Declarer played ace and another heart, ruffing in hand, then three rounds of trumps. Since East still had a trump, the slam was one down.

"Sorry about my lead," said Brother Aelred, much relieved that the slam had failed anyway. "My aces always seem to get ruffed nowadays."

"No, no. It was an exceptionally good lead," replied Brother Lucius. "The only lead to threaten the contract, in fact."

"Yes, it was quite a fair defence," commented the Abbot, "but I must say I would have left the double in on your cards, Brother Rupert."

"Well, the spade slam can still be made actually, Abbot," said Brother Lucius. "After the knave of clubs is allowed to hold, declarer can ruff the clubs good, ruff the hearts good, cash the three top trumps and run the clubs. East can make his trump when he likes but the dummy is now high."

"Yes, yes. Anyone can see that," snapped the Abbot. "In my view, though, a substantial penalty above the line is a better prospect than a pie-in-the-sky slam that may prove beyond declarer's abilities."

Brother Rupert gazed at the eleven tricks stacked before him, waiting for the storm to abate.

"Well, I can't stand here all day. Some of us have work to do," declared the Abbot. "A good day to you all."

"Phew! That was a close one," said Brother Rupert, passing a rather gay blue and white handkerchief over his perspiring forehead. "Was my six spade call as bad as all that?"

"Of course it wasn't," Brother Lucius smiled back. "After all, you could hardly leave spades unmentioned. You had a royal flush!"

33

Escape from St. Titus

Brother Aelred and Brother Michael leapt boldly down from the dangerously high monastery outer wall, retrieved their bicycles and pedalled silently towards Hursley Village. Tonight was the Charity Simultaneous Pairs and the two monks, who would have little hope in the strong monastery heat, were heading for a somewhat greener pasture.

"It feels really strange wearing a suit again," said Brother Aelred, as they walked apprehensively into Hursley village hall. "Does my tie look all right?"

"Ah, two new boys, how nice!" exclaimed Mrs. Port-Binding, looking up from her cashbox with a welcoming smile. "That will be £1 each, please. Just 20p for expenses, the rest for charity. If you take a seat over there at table 5 you can play the first round against myself and Mrs. Nutbeam."

The hall was unusually noisy but Brother Aelred was able to distinguish odd snatches of conversation.

"What, Iris Boyes? Never. She must be well into her forties."

"Yes, 4 lb. of Seville oranges, and I always add . . ."

". . . and according to Mrs. Cottell, the light was off for almost twenty minutes."

Suddenly Brother Aelred felt immensely confident. Why, in all probability he and Brother Michael were the only club masters in the whole room. What a refreshing change from the monastery, where three lifemasters paraded their skills and regional masters were two a penny.

Escape from St. Titus

N–S game, dealer North

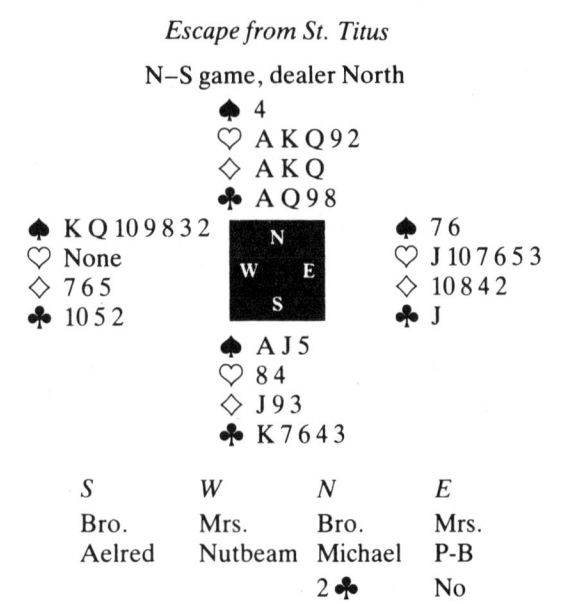

```
              ♠ 4
              ♡ A K Q 9 2
              ♢ A K Q
              ♣ A Q 9 8
♠ K Q 10 9 8 3 2            ♠ 7 6
♡ None                     ♡ J 10 7 6 5 3
♢ 7 6 5                    ♢ 10 8 4 2
♣ 10 5 2                   ♣ J
              ♠ A J 5
              ♡ 8 4
              ♢ J 9 3
              ♣ K 7 6 4 3
```

S	W	N	E
Bro.	Mrs.	Bro.	Mrs.
Aelred	Nutbeam	Michael	P-B
		2 ♣	No
2 NT	3 ♠	6 ♡	dble
6 NT	End		

Brother Michael had a difficult bid over Mrs. Nutbeam's three spades. A more sophisticated player would probably have passed at this point. When Mrs. Port-Binding doubled in a voice of thunder, Brother Aelred was glad of an excuse to transfer to 6 NT.

The king of spades was led, and Brother Aelred fingered his saffron bow-tie as he inspected the dummy. There were twelve tricks on top, barring a 4–0 break in clubs. Brother Aelred recalled the ominous words of a well-known tome: "Assume that the cards lie badly and consider possible counter-measures."

If clubs were 4–0, extra tricks would be needed from somewhere. With this in mind, Brother Aelred ducked the opening lead. Winning the diamond switch, he cashed the ace, queen and king of clubs, then observed that the club suit had somehow become blocked. After much thought Brother Aelred solved the problem by throwing dummy's last club on the ace of spades and running the rest of the suit.

"Beautifully played, partner," exclaimed Brother Michael. "How did you spot that hold-up play?"

"Oh, it's in all the books," replied Brother Aelred. "We're jolly

lucky seven clubs doesn't make, though. They can take a heart ruff."

"Was it wise to double six hearts, Gloria?" enquired Mrs. Nutbeam. "If six hearts is passed out, we get a lovely top."

"That may be," replied Mrs. Port-Binding. "But it's a funny game if I'm not allowed to double a slam when I hold six trumps and you've bid up to the three-level on your own hand."

Swept along by a strong current of opponents' errors, the monastery pair continued to shine. Brother Michael estimated their score at an unprecedented 70 per cent when, sitting West against two bearded students on the last hand of the evening, he picked up the following hand:

♠ A Q 10 5
♡ A 5
♢ A 6 5 2
♣ 8 5 3

North opened one club and South responded one spade.

"No bid," said Brother Michael, pleased that his spades seemed to be sitting well.

North raised to two spades and South, whose reddish beard clashed oddly with his orange tee-shirt, bid a third.

"Bid four spades!" wished Brother Michael, directing every ounce of available will power leftwards.

"Four spades," said North obediently.

Brother Michael doubled and led the ace of hearts. When the dummy went down, he saw to his annoyance that it contained both the missing spade honours.

Game all, dealer North

```
                    ♠ K J 6 2
                    ♡ K Q
                    ♢ 8 4 3
                    ♣ A J 10 6
  ♠ A Q 10 5                        ♠ None
  ♡ A 5           N                 ♡ 10 9 7 6 4 3 2
  ♢ A 6 5 2     W   E               ♢ J 10 9
  ♣ 8 5 3         S                 ♣ Q 7 2
                    ♠ 9 8 7 4 3
                    ♡ J 8
                    ♢ K Q 7
                    ♣ K 9 4
```

S	W	N	E
Bearded	Bro.	Bearded	Bro.
Student	Michael	Student	Aelred
		1 ♣	No
1 ♠	No	2 ♠	No
3 ♠	No	4 ♠	No
No	dble	End	

Declarer won the second heart in dummy and led the six of clubs. Brother Aelred, sitting East, glared at this card suspiciously. Was declarer leading towards ♣ 9 x, hoping that West, the safe hand, would win? Yes, that must be it. Up with the queen and fire a diamond through!

South captured the club queen, looking none too pleased. Short of a necessary entry for the deep finesse in spades, he finished one down.

"Man, that was some defence!" he gasped, staring at Brother Aelred open-mouthed. "If you don't stick the club queen in, it's 790s-ville for sure. Club nine wins, spade through, back to the club king and another spade finishes it."

"You seem to know what you're talking about," commented Brother Michael. "Do you live locally?"

"No, we hitched from London actually," said North, filling in the scoreslip. "We often play Charities here. Not much opposition, as a rule."

"True. We're not local either," confided Brother Aelred with a sly smile, proceeding to inspect the student's scorecard in life-masterly fashion. "Oh, I see you beat 6 NT on board 17."

"Board 17?" replied the other student. "Yes, that was amusing. I led the king of spades and . . ."

"But surely the lead makes no difference," interrupted Brother Aelred expertly, "unless . . . Oh no! You're not going to tell me someone missed the Bath Coup, are you?"

34

The Condemnation of Brother Anthony

The Abbot unlatched the front door of his Lodge, and in from a howling gale came Brother Lucius, his cassock drenched and his hair in windswept disarray.

"Good grief!" exclaimed the Abbot. "What appalling weather for September! Come and warm yourself by the fire."

Restoring his hair to comparative respectability, Brother Lucius walked over to the fire and gazed gratefully down at the crackling logs.

"Here, have a glass of mulled wine," offered the Abbot. "It's quite a strong brew. Now, who did you manage to get for a fourth tonight?"

"Well, it wasn't easy to find anyone, with the Manchester United replay on TV tonight, but eventually I persuaded Brother Anthony to play again."

"Oh . . . er . . . good," replied the Abbot unconvincingly.

A member of the silent Eustacian order, Brother Anthony was not the most popular of partners. Only the previous week a young and impecunious postulant, on cutting Brother Anthony, had feigned an acute cramp and hobbled off to the infirmary.

"Have a gander outside the door," said the Abbot, pouring out some more drinks. "Perhaps Brother Anthony has arrived."

Brother Lucius opened the door and the tall figure of Brother Anthony entered, his customary smile undampened by the rain. He had always regarded knocking on a door as contrary to his vow of silence, and his friends were forever looking outside their doors in case he was proposing to pay them a visit.

When Brother Xavier arrived only five minutes late, which was early for him, the four was complete.

Love all, dealer West

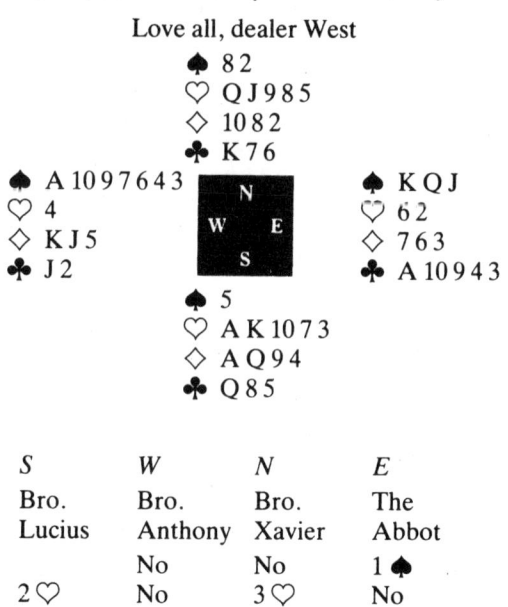

♠ 82
♡ Q J 9 8 5
◇ 10 8 2
♣ K 7 6

♠ A 10 9 7 6 4 3
♡ 4
◇ K J 5
♣ J 2

♠ K Q J
♡ 6 2
◇ 7 6 3
♣ A 10 9 4 3

♠ 5
♡ A K 10 7 3
◇ A Q 9 4
♣ Q 8 5

S	W	N	E
Bro.	Bro.	Bro.	The
Lucius	Anthony	Xavier	Abbot
	No	No	1 ♠
2 ♡	No	3 ♡	No
4 ♡	End		

The Abbot made a lead-directing bid of one spade in third position and Brother Lucius, who had an obvious take-out double at his disposal, opted instead for a rather selfish heart overcall. Defending against four hearts, Brother Anthony led the ace of spades and switched to the knave of clubs.

Since the Abbot had bid spades only at the one-level, always a suspect manoeuvre with a Eustacian partner, and had shown no sign of considering a spade sacrifice, Brother Lucius was inclined to place most of the spade length with West. Deciding therefore to play East for the club length, he covered the knave of clubs with the king, compelling the Abbot to win the trick.

Declarer won the club return, drew trumps and eliminated spades. He then ran the eight of diamonds to West's knave and captured the forced diamond exit with dummy's ten. Three trump tricks were taken and a diamond was led from the table at trick 12. When the Abbot followed small in the East seat, his last card was known to be a club. Brother Lucius therefore went up with the ace, dropping West's king, and claimed the contract.

[157]

"Well, I certainly picked the right suit to bid," said the Abbot ruefully. "If only I'd been bold enough to call it at the four-level we could have made game ourselves!"

Brother Lucius refrained from pointing out that a diamond return at trick 3 would have beaten the heart game, so play proceeded. On the next hand the Abbot made a Eustacian Gambling 3 NT opening on a balanced 15-count and scored four overtricks when Brother Anthony provided a 21-point dummy. It was still game all in the first rubber when the following hand arrived.

Game all, dealer South

```
              ♠ 8 7 5 2
              ♡ 7 4
              ◇ A 10 6
              ♣ K Q J 4
  ♠ 10 4                        ♠ K Q J 9
  ♡ 8 3          N              ♡ J 5 2
  ◇ 9 8 7 4   W     E           ◇ K Q 2
  ♣ A 10 9 7 2    S             ♣ 8 5 3
              ♠ A 6 3
              ♡ A K Q 10 9 6
              ◇ J 5 3
              ♣ 6
```

S	W	N	E
The	Bro.	Bro.	Bro.
Abbot	Lucius	Anthony	Xavier
4 ♡	No	No	No

The Abbot once more gave some consideration to a 3 NT opening on the South cards, but nine tricks was a narrow target and the honours tilted his decision towards the heart game.

Brother Lucius led the nine of diamonds to his partner's queen and the king of spades was returned. The Abbot ducked once and took the spade continuation. After drawing trumps he led a club towards the dummy. Brother Lucius did his best by ducking, but the Abbot simply won in the dummy and played a second club honour, discarding a loser from hand.

"Not the best," muttered Brother Lucius. This was his usual phrase when a defence had gone astray.